Geor

George Altman

My Baseball Journey
from the Negro Leagues
to the Majors and Beyond

GEORGE ALTMAN
with Lew Freedman

McFarland & Company, Inc., Publishers
Jefferson, North Carolina, and London

All photographs courtesy of George Altman

Library of Congress Cataloguing-in-Publication Data

Altman, George, 1933–
    George Altman : my baseball journey from the Negro
leagues to the Majors and beyond / George Altman
with Lew Freedman.
        p.   cm.
    Includes bibliographical references and index.

    ISBN 978-0-7864-7103-4
    softcover : acid free paper ∞

    1. Altman, George, 1933–   2. African American baseball
players—Biography.   3. Baseball players—United States—
Biography.   I. Freedman, Lew.   II. Title.
GV865.A44A3 2013
796.357092—dc23
[B]   2013029113

British Library cataloguing data are available

Front cover: George Altman of the Chicago Cubs (National
Baseball Hall of Fame Library Cooperstown, New York)
Back cover: Altman (see arrow) as a member of the Tokyo/
Lotte Orions.

Manufactured in the United States of America

McFarland & Company, Inc., Publishers
    Box 611, Jefferson, North Carolina 28640
    www.mcfarlandpub.com

I would like to dedicate this book first of all to God who gave me the talent and strength to persevere through all of my adversities and setbacks.

Also to my mother, whom I never really knew. Everyone who knew her said that she was a beautiful, kind and loving person. I have tried to use her legacy as a guideline for my life.

And to my wonderful and loving wife Etta, to my children, relatives and friends who gave me love, comfort and support.

I am grateful and thankful to my coaches, Cash, McLendon, Simmons, Whitmon, and especially Buck O'Neil.

Table of Contents

Table of Contents

Introduction by Lew Freedman

George Altman had the most diverse baseball career of anyone who ever played the game.

Altman, who was born in Goldsboro, North Carolina, in 1933, not only played the game as a youth, but he competed at Tennessee State University, while in the United States Army, for the Kansas City Monarchs in the old Negro Leagues, in the minors, and in winter ball in Panama and Cuba. He spent nearly a decade in the majors with the Chicago Cubs, St. Louis Cardinals, and New York Mets, and also became one of the early former big-leaguers to play in Japan. Wherever they rolled out the bats and balls, George Altman was not far behind. With the Monarchs, Altman played for the legendary Buck O'Neil as his manager. Rangy and quick-wristed at the plate, Altman was twice named a National League All-Star with the Cubs. Later, he extended his career by playing eight seasons in Japan, most of them with the Tokyo Orions but also with the Hanshin Tigers.

Altman was nicknamed "Big George." His 6-foot-4 height also made him a superb basketball player earlier in life, and he suggests that despite his all-around success in baseball that hoops may even have been his best sport.

After retiring from baseball, Altman chose racquetball as his favorite sport for conditioning and competition. He played competitively for more than 20 years and won a few trophies. More recently, he moved on to horseshoes, an endeavor he calls much less strenuous. Altman has continued to compete in that sport and has won tournaments in his age division.

Among his variety of achievements in the majors, Altman saved a no-hitter with the Cubs with a ninth-inning outfield catch, led the

1

National League in triples, hit a pinch-hit home run in the All-Star Game, and in a rarity given the Hall of Fame pitcher's wizardry at the time, Altman hit two home runs in one game off Sandy Koufax. A different kind of accomplishment was becoming at least semi-conversant in Japanese.

Only a few major leaguers of a certain age passed through the Negro Leagues before they reached the majors and also experimented with playing in Japan. No one else, however, also played college baseball and service ball, minor-leagues, and winter ball, besides Altman. His was a unique baseball career, one that began in neighborhood play, just like that of millions of other little boys before Little League became an official option.

Altman actually attended Tennessee State, then an NAIA school, on a basketball scholarship, though as a youth he started playing baseball first. Being tall helped direct Altman to the hardwood, and being in school already helped redirect him to the baseball diamond again.

Almost no one in Altman's family participated in sports during his youth, so he had to find his own way. He came from a family of automobile mechanics, not outfielders or dribblers. When Altman went off to college in Tennessee he thought he might become a high school basketball coach when he finished, or go into the business field if the opportunity came along.

A mutual friend connected Altman to the Monarchs, one of the signature franchises of the Negro Leagues, which were then fading out since the majors had committed to integration. Altman spent enough time with the gracious, informative, and wise Buck O'Neil to get a head start in the game.

Very briefly, during one of his stretches with the Monarchs, Satchel Paige dazzled the young Altman, too. "I felt like I was playing on hallowed ground," Altman said of sharing a field with the legendary Paige, perhaps the greatest pitcher who ever lived. "To be on the same team as Satchel Paige and sit around listening to him tell stories was pretty special. I had heard so much about him and the older guys."

Altman's short association with O'Neil in Kansas City paid dividends. As the venerable Monarchs disappeared, O'Neil joined the Chicago Cubs as a scout (and later became the majors' first African American coach with the team). O'Neil recommended several black play-

George Altman signing an autograph at a Negro Leagues Museum function in Kansas City.

ers to the Cubs who had played together on the 1955 Monarchs, and Altman, Lou Johnson and J. C. Hartman all signed and made the majors.

It was not for big money. Laughing as he told the tale, Altman said the Wrigleys, the team owners, did not exactly pay large bonuses.

"We got a pack of chewing gum from Wrigley," Altman joked.

By the time he got out of the Army and made an impression in the minors, Altman was already 26 years old. In spring training of 1959, Altman came to camp with a AAA contract. But he hit very well, smacking line drives all over the complex and batting about .340. He also possessed more speed than almost anyone else around and out-raced other guys regularly. Manager Bob Scheffing liked the look of the hard-hitting outfielder and asked Altman if he could play center field. Naturally, he said yes because he wasn't going to pass up an opportunity, though he had only dabbled in center field as a youth.

When it came time for Altman's major league debut, the Cubs

opened the season at home in venerable Wrigley Field. However, in keeping with Chicago's irregular brand of weather, snow flakes fell during Altman's first game against the Los Angeles Dodgers as part of the opening day décor.

Altman was fairly successful dodging snowfall that day, in a game played in 42-degree temperatures, but was less successful dodging the fastballs thrown by future Hall of Fame right-hander Don Drysdale, who was known for brushing hitters back. On the first pitch of Altman's major league career, he was struck by a Drysdale fastball. Altman's clearest memory of the first game of his big-league career was not any bruise incurred from Drysdale's errant pitch, though. He just remembers hoping that every day in Chicago wouldn't be so cold.

That began Altman's solid major league career, sharing experiences with such famous Cubs as Ernie Banks, Ron Santo, and Billy Williams.

Less expected for a man who played baseball in several countries, at several levels of the sport, was the pleasant continuation of his career in Japan at a time when few Americans took the leap. Altman became a cross-cultural home-run-hitting star, and across the ocean even played for another team whose ownership produced chewing gum.

As far as baseball odysseys go, Altman's was unrivaled. It also means that he has baseball connections all over the world. He stays in touch with various teammates he met while playing in so many places. In the summer of 2012, Altman was invited to appear at a special program at the Negro Leagues Museum in Kansas City, where the Major League All-Star game was being played. At the time he was one of seven living former Negro Leagues players who had been selected as a major league all-star.

George Altman's baseball journey has been a special one and a long one. The only remaining baseball goal he would like to see fulfilled is for the Cubs to win the World Series in his lifetime. Although he lives much closer to St. Louis than to Chicago, the Cubs still own his heart. They gave him his first break in the majors and as Altman likes to say, once a Cub, always a Cub.

"I'm pulling for them," Altman said.

I first met George Altman on the telephone to interview him about his days with the Chicago Cubs. The more we talked, the more I was fascinated by his incredible baseball career. I had never heard of anyone who had played baseball at so many different levels. The more I thought about it the more I realized it would be a treat to hear all about it, to hear all the stories from the past — and to share them with baseball fans.

That led to the collaboration on this book, a joint effort between a curious fan and an old ballplayer. At the top of each chapter, leading into each step of George's journey, I provide a context of the times, the league, the team, or simply what was going on in baseball. Then George takes over in his first-person voice.

1

Growing Up in Goldsboro

George Lee Altman was born on March 20, 1933. The future outfielder's place of birth was a small town in North Carolina. Goldsboro, which was incorporated in 1847, today has about 38,000 people and is located in the eastern half of the state in Wayne County, about an hour southeast of the state capital of Raleigh.

During the Civil War, the battle of Goldsborough Bridge was fought in the area and the Union Army destroyed the railroad bridge that provided a connection to Wilmington. A notoriously warm and muggy climate is characteristic of the summer months — the baseball-playing months — in Goldsboro.

Among the notable people who either were born in Goldsboro or lived there are actor Andy Griffith, golfer Mark O'Meara, Jimmy Graham, a star tight end for the New Orleans Saints, major league baseball managers Clyde King and Jerry Narron — and George Altman.

During Altman's youth the economy relied most heavily on farming, with some manufacturing in the area. As in so much of North Carolina, tobacco was a major cash crop.

My father's name was Willie Altman and my mother was named Clara. My father was a tenant farmer in a little town called Seven Springs, but my mother died of pneumonia when I was only four years old. I think it was pneumonia. My father was not one to talk much about things, so I really wasn't sure what the cause of death was.

Goldsboro was mostly farming. Tobacco was big. There used to be more cotton. There was also a furniture factory. Seymour Johnson Field Air Force Base was there and a state mental institution is still there.

I was an only child and it was hard to grow up without a mother.

Much later, when I was 40, I found out I had a half-brother. Some cousins mentioned it and my father finally admitted to that.

For about a year after my mother died I lived with an aunt, my father's sister Lena. But then my father got married again and I had a stepmother, Rosa Altman. The three of us lived in a small house, the kind that they used to call a shotgun house that was straight from the front to the back. It was a three-room house. It had two bedrooms and a kitchen. My father made his money as a tenant farmer, which means he worked someone else's land. He raised cotton and tobacco. He wasn't much of a farmer and moved to Goldsboro when my mother died to begin his career as an auto mechanic.

I was interested in sports from the time I was just a youngster. Right from the beginning. I played with the other kids from the neighborhood, especially in the summer. There was an elementary school near where we lived and it had a playground. I was at that playground whenever I had the opportunity. All day long, if I could be there.

In a way it was what we would think of as an all-around summer recreation program for kids so they kept busy with something to do when school was out. Actually, if I remember correctly, it opened in the afternoon, maybe one o'clock, and stayed open until about six o'clock. They had games like checkers and horseshoes. They didn't have table games. When the playground was closed we played marbles and hop-scotch.

For me the most important thing was the competition. I always liked competition. I guess I was born with that in me because I otherwise don't know where it came from. I can't think of anyone else who influenced me like that. There would be different kids at the playground every day, but I was there every day.

In those days every little community had a baseball team that represented the town. In Goldsboro, the white and black neighborhoods were separate. The dividing line was Williams Street, and I remember that right across the street from Williams Street was a baseball diamond. It was the whites' baseball diamond. That's where the cotton mill team played. They had uniforms and played with shiny balls, all that kind of new equipment. It was a team of all-white players, but we could go over and watch. That was my first exposure to baseball.

I was too young, but I couldn't have played on that team, anyway, because I was black. A little bit later Goldsboro got a minor league team. It was called the Goldsboro Goldbugs. The team had actually played for one year in 1929 in the Eastern Carolina League, but it didn't last. Then, when I was a little kid it came back with the same name, starting in 1937. But then it was in the Coastal Plain League. This was Class D, the lowest level of the minors.

The Goldbugs. That was the nickname of the team. I became a fan of the team and they had a big first baseman named Jack Hussey. He was a really good hitter and he was my first baseball idol. He didn't make it to the majors, but he was a local star.

To tell you the truth, we didn't have the money to go to the games, so I mostly listened to the Goldbugs play on the radio. I used to sit on the back porch and listen to the ballgames and imagine how the guys looked.

When I first began playing baseball as a kid, none of us had money for real equipment. We used paper sacks for gloves. Brown paper bags. We couldn't afford real baseballs, either, so we played catch using potatoes. I'll tell you if you threw a potato it would really pop when you caught it. You'd think you were throwing it amazingly fast. You'd think, "Boy, I'm firing this ball in here!" We made our own bats, too. We used broomsticks for our bats and we used pop bottle tops for the balls that we hit. One thing about the pop bottle thing was that it went into a big curve when you threw it. That way all of the kids in my neighborhood ended up knowing how to hit the curveball. They got that ability from that experience. The pop bottle tops were little, about the size of a golf ball, maybe. So that definitely developed your batting eye.

W. Clement Stone, founder of Combined Insurance Company of America and a fellow board member of the Woodlawn Boys Club in Chicago, used to say that out of every adversity there comes an equal or greater benefit. We didn't have the proper equipment, so the benefit was learning how to hit the curveball. That was really valuable because not being able to hit the curveball is what separated the best hitters from those who couldn't get beyond the minors. Not hitting the curve is what got a lot of guys sent home from pro ball. It still does. "Mom, I'm doing OK, but they're starting to throw the curveball. I'll be home soon."

I was in elementary school, roughly from ages eight to 11, when I was playing with broomsticks and bottle caps. But our elementary school also had a soft-pitch baseball team and I played on that team. I found out fairly early that I had a little bit of talent. There was a ditch in right field, not far beyond the infield diamond, and then there were houses beyond that. Most of the guys were trying to hit the ball as far as the ditch and I was hitting the ball over to the houses. I would hit the ball off the sides of the houses. I didn't break any windows, though.

It was tremendous, a tremendous thing, when I discovered that I was pretty good at playing baseball. We lived in the North End, and the North End of Goldsboro had a team. There were three sandlot teams. The North End, the East End and the West End all had teams. The whites-only mill team was like semi-pro compared to us.

The name of my team was North End. We used to play games against the East End and the West End and then our schedule broadened. North Carolina is made up of a bunch of small towns, and every 15 miles or so down the road is another town. They all had teams. We played against Mount Olive, Snow Hill, Park Town. There were also the Jason Tigers. They were so good they were like semi-pro. That was the kind of team that a touring Negro Leagues team would play against in an exhibition when they came through.

After I played with North End, I played for the White Oak team on weekends. I was big for my age and that was true by the time I was 12 or 13. By the time I was 14 or 15 I started playing more with teams that had grown men and were a little bit farther away from home. The Park Town team was next for me, and they were called the Park Town Parkers or something like that. They played Jason and other towns. It was better competition.

The Jason Tigers were made up of all grown men and although we played against them once in a while, they were out of our league. They had guys on that team that I imagine had gone away and played some ball and then settled back in town.

From the time I was young, even before high school age, I also had to work. We lived in a farming community and that's where the work was. They used to hire a lot of day laborers. A truck would come by through the neighborhood looking to pick up people to go harvest beans and tobacco and pick cotton. We might ride about 20 miles to the fields and there might be six, seven or eight of us on a truck. The truck was like a little pickup truck.

It wasn't my idea to work. It was my father's suggestion, and my stepmother's. They said things like if I wanted to eat or wanted to buy a new pair of shoes I should work. I was about 14 when I started doing that type of labor. I didn't like it because it cut into my playground time. Of course all of the other guys were working, too, so that limited our primary baseball playing time to the weekends.

My father didn't talk much at all. He believed in hard work, but he was not the type of man to talk much about his feelings, his past, or even his family. I never even knew who my paternal grandfather was until I was 40 years old. I was related to one of the biggest families in town, the Barneses, and I had a lot of cousins. In fact, some of the girls were in my same class and I didn't even know. I was kind of sweet on a couple of them. We didn't date, but we almost did. My father always thought sports were frivolous. He didn't picture anyone making a living out of playing sports. He never saw me play in high school or in college. Later, he watched some of my baseball games on TV. He didn't go to those games, either, and no, he never really told me he was proud of me.

I don't know what it was. He was a tough nut. He was a macho guy. People in town sometimes told stories about my father related to when he was working as an auto mechanic. They said he picked up the car himself and didn't use a jack. He wasn't that big of a guy, maybe 190 pounds, and he wasn't as tall as I was. He was very strong, though. When the circus came to town, he might have been the only local guy wrestling the bears. I don't know if he won. Probably not. I just heard the story. I'd hear guys talk about it, but I never saw him do it.

Those were long, hot days, hard days, working in the fields. Summer in North Carolina can be brutally hot and humid. I still remember how it felt. That experience also convinced me that I did not want to make a career out of picking cotton or working in the fields if I could help it. That taught me that there had to be something better out there for me. It also made school look a little bit better to me.

Picking cotton is a lot of work. You are always bending. Sometimes we used to crawl as we picked it. That wasn't too good for the knees. You'd start early in the morning when it was a little bit cooler. But it got hot quickly enough. There was moisture, dew, on the crop early in the morning. That was one incentive to start early because we got paid by the pound and the cotton was heavier in early morning. The more cotton you picked during that time, before it dried out, you got paid more because the cotton weighed more.

I can't remember exactly how much we got paid, but it could have been 30 cents a pound. The goal was to pick 100 pounds. That was everybody's goal, to pick 100 pounds in a day so you could make maybe $3 or $4 for a day's pay. It was good money at the time. That was all you had as a kid.

I began doing that in my early teen years and I did it for three or four summers. Then, when I got a little bit older, later in my teens, a group from my high school used to travel to Connecticut every year to harvest tobacco. It was broad leaf tobacco, probably for cigars. They imported workers. It was far away from home, but it was great because everybody lived in a house. It was like a dormitory with other kids and we got paid a lot more than we got paid in North Carolina. I guess they figured that we were tobacco experts because we came from tobacco country.

We used to knock off work about four or five o'clock, when it was still light, and we had a quick dinner and then played ball. Sometimes we played horseshoes, sometimes baseball, and sometimes softball. It was good competition. We used to play softball against a local team. It was a white team, but they didn't care. They were older players, but we held our own.

The Connecticut team had a guy named Lefty who was the first baseman. He was kind of small in stature, but he could hit the ball a long way. Beyond right field they had a tobacco barn and he tried to hit the ball high and deep to the barn and he did it more than anybody else. I used to do it sometimes. That was the whole thing, to see if you could hit it over the barn. I think he won, but I was right there. They actually wanted me to come play for their team sometimes, but I couldn't do that because of our work schedule and because they went out of town to play.

Although I was a pretty good athlete, my father didn't care about sports at all. He didn't give me any instruction or really any encouragement. He wanted me to quit playing ball and go to work. The whole time that I played football, basketball and baseball in high school he never saw a game. He never went.

I had to learn how to play my sports by watching others. The soft-pitch team in elementary school was my first real exposure. That was an all African American school. All of the schools were segregated and the town was divided. I never played with white kids on the playground. I never knew them at all. I never crossed paths with them. We didn't live far away from the white high school, but I never really knew exactly where it was. I never saw them in the streets and my family never took a newspaper, so I didn't even keep up with what they were doing.

At the same time I never felt any discrimination. We stayed in our area. The only time I might run into white people was when I had a paper route and delivered the newspaper in the morning. I did that in grammar school and most of those newspapers were delivered in white neighborhoods. That was probably the only contact with whites I had. It was sort of like having two worlds with them never overlapping. Same thing with being poor. One of my buddies said, "You know, we were poor, but we didn't even know it." That's because everyone was in the same boat. But we were poor and I knew it, definitely so.

If we weren't poor I would have been able to afford to buy a baseball glove. I think I asked my father for a baseball glove for Christmas, but I didn't get one. Christmas, especially during World War II, was pretty Spartan. We might have some fruit as a treat and maybe we got some firecrackers. I was born during the Depression and I was a kid during World War II. It was kind of a tough time. Everything was being rationed.

You know, I don't even remember my first baseball glove. It was not a gift from anyone in my family and it was not a new glove. I think my first glove was a hand-me-down from a manager who purchased a new glove and let me have his old one. I was probably 12 or so, junior high age. It wasn't like my own special possession that I took care of and broke in from the time it was new. I never had one of those.

When I first began playing baseball I was one of the younger players, and some of the other young players had older brothers who looked out for them. If I wanted to play I had to play a position that no one else did, so the first thing I played was catcher. When I grew a little bit I became a shortstop and then I moved to center field.

My freshman year in high school at Dillard High School was 1947, right after the war, when I was 14. There were a lot of teams of older guys, returning veterans, playing games against the high school clubs. We were playing in a town called Rocky Mount that had one of those old parks with a tin fence around it. I was sitting on the bench and the

13

coach was looking around trying to decide who to put in as a hitter. There were a couple of runners on base, but our team hadn't been hitting at all. The assistant coach said to the coach, "Put that Altman kid in and let him hit. He can hit." I was shaking I was so nervous. It was one of the first games of the season and I hadn't played yet at all. So I went up to the plate and I got lucky. I hit the ball off the fence and to this day I can remember the sound that ball made, BAM! I got to play more after that. It was a double or a triple and so they put me in again. I was hitting.

It's funny. There were a lot of teams named the Tigers around me. The Jason Tigers. The Dillard Tigers. And the Raleigh Tigers were a professional team, one of the teams that played against the touring Negro Leagues teams when they came to North Carolina.

Then in college we were the Tennessee State Tigers. As an aside, Buck Leonard, a member of the Baseball Hall of Fame, lived and died in Rocky Mount, North Carolina, where my baseball journey basically started.

I played four years of baseball in high school between 1947 and 1951, the year I graduated. I also played two years of basketball for Dillard. Most of the guys in the North End played baseball. The community center that had a gym was in the West End. Those guys were territorial and they didn't want to allow us to play there. We didn't go over there much. We mostly stayed in our neighborhoods.

Sooner or later, because I was a bigger kid, and I had no older brothers, I had to learn how to fight. Kids always bothered you if they thought they could. One would start it and another would jump in. Then they brought their big brother in. I had to learn early that if I didn't fight they would keep picking on me. I held my own. I had to run sometimes and I remember one day one of the guys' brothers came along. I had never started a fight. That wasn't in my nature.

But this time I knew the older brother was coming after me. I don't even remember the cause. But I hit him before he could hit me and then I took off running. They were both chasing me and they threw a brick at me. I ran all of the way home and I ran right in the door and the brick came in the door right after me — through the open door. It was that close. They didn't break anything. Nobody else was home to say anything. My stepmother worked in a factory and by then my father was working as an automobile mechanic.

That was not the end of it, of course. I had to fight with them and I did pretty well so they started leaving me alone. By my sophomore year in high school I grew quite a bit and was probably about six-foot-three by then. That was big for those days. That's when I decided I wanted to play basketball. The only games that mattered were in the West End, across town. I rode my bicycle over there and the first day I parked it outside the gym and when I came out of course it was gone. I had to fight again and run home. It was about two-and-a-half or three miles.

I hadn't expected that my bike would be stolen on the first day, but after I thought about it, it was kind of, "Well, what did you expect?" But I couldn't replace it. I ended up running back and forth between home and that gym and I think that helped me with my speed and stamina. I ended up being a pretty fast runner. At that height in that era I became a center and I was not only tall, but a good player, so everyone wanted me on their team. I didn't have to fight anymore.

I was mostly an inside player, a good rebounder, strong underneath the basket. But if I got the ball I was like a lot of the other guys and I just shot it. It might be 30 feet from the basket.

Actually, I had always been interested in basketball. There was a goal set up at the elementary school and that's where I learned to shoot. Most of the time I was out there by myself and I was out there a lot. The goal didn't have any strings on it. It was just a metal hoop.

I also started playing football in high school, and that was because of the neighborhood guys I spent the summer with in Connecticut. A lot of them were football players and they were my friends, so I went out for the team. I became an end. You played both ways then, so I played offensive and defensive end. I was tall and rangy and I could catch the ball and run. I could run like the wind at that time. I played two years of high school football. We had good teams. We made the playoffs and we won a divisional title. We had a good defensive team. When we won the divisional title we won, 6–0. I caught a touchdown pass for the only points.

Our basketball team was very good, too. We qualified for the state playoffs my senior year, but I got the flu and they had to drag me to the game out of my bed. I remember that I was so sick that I had to lie down on the bus on the way over there. I would play a couple of minutes, come out and rest on the bench and maybe throw up, then go back in. We lost our last game by one or two points.

The whole time I was in high school, all of the competition was segregated. We never played against white schools at all. My teammates were all black. We had a winning tradition at Dillard High School. We were highly competitive in and winners in football, basketball and baseball. We very much would have liked to have played against the white high school in our town and other white high schools in our area.

In the years since then I have often thought about how strange the world was back then when everything was segregated. We live in a very different society now.

2

Basketball at Tennessee State

After graduating from high school in North Carolina in 1951, George Altman was surprised to learn that he was coveted more for his basketball skills than his baseball skills. He was sought after to play basketball at Tennessee State, which was founded as Tennessee A&I.

Even Altman's ability as a football player was stressed above his capabilities on the diamond. Altman was steered to Tennessee State in Nashville by a local benefactor in his home town. George Wilson was a businessman who had a close association with an athletic figure at Tennessee State from his own college days.

Altman had not heard of Tennessee State, nor had he ever visited Nashville. The world of college sports recruiting was far different from what it is now. It was not very sophisticated. Even the best teams tended either to sign up local athletes or the coaches relied on the word of trusted friends that an individual athlete could play well enough to help his team and would be a good enough student to make the grade.

Coaches did not have recruiting budgets that allowed them to travel to other states, and there were no published recruiting newsletters and bulletins to spread knowledge around about individual athletes, especially those from small towns.

During the 1950s, an invitation to campus did not always mean that a player was going to be a member of the team, or that he was guaranteed a scholarship. It might only mean that the coach was willing to take a look at a player in a tryout. So in the late summer of 1951, Altman packed his suitcase and made his way to Nashville for what amounted to a basketball tryout.

When I was growing up in Goldsboro, I used to listen to college basketball on the radio. I listened to the North Carolina games and the

17

Duke games. I used to listen to them and wish I could go play against them.

When I was directed to Tennessee State that was exciting for me because it meant I could go to college; otherwise I couldn't afford it. In those days what passed for a scholarship was work aid. It meant they gave you a job so you could afford your tuition, your meals and your living expenses.

Nashville was a big city compared to Goldsboro. Tennessee State didn't really have much of a gym, but it was bigger than the one Dillard played its games in. It wasn't a fancy place, but it was an upgrade over my high school gym. The gym wasn't large enough for our fans and student body so we couldn't play our home games in it. We played our home ballgames at Fisk University. Fisk, which was just down the street, had a new gym that held a few thousand people.

The biggest surprise for me when I got to Tennessee State was that it seemed as if the basketball coach, Clarence Cash, had invited everyone in the world to his summer camp to try out for the team. There were about ten guys there from Chicago and there were a half-dozen from Tennessee. The coach's son had brought some friends along. There were at least three guys from Nashville and the rest were from the area. I think there were about 40 guys there trying out for the team. They were probably all asked to come with the idea that they were going to play basketball. It turned out we had to fight for a place on the team. At the time I went into college I was a better basketball player than baseball player.

Being a traditionally black school, Tennessee State was able to recruit many of the top African American basketball players in the country. At the time a lot of white schools still wouldn't recruit any black basketball players, and most of them might only want one or two. The National Invitational Interscholastic Basketball Tournament, a championship tournament for black high school teams, was conducted in Nashville at Fisk. That meant that all of the best players came to Nashville and all the Tennessee State coaches had to do was show up on campus down the street to see them. It was as convenient as it could be.

They put the word out that the good players were encouraged to try out for the team. They had seen them play, so they could invite the best. You had to have some credentials, but they invited way more players than they could use. The tryouts were cut-throat because so much was at stake. This was a lifetime opportunity because not many of us could afford to attend college on our own.

It was definitely every man for himself on the court. A guy like me had trouble getting anyone to pass the ball to him. The Chicago guys only passed the ball to other Chicago guys. Everyone was trying to impress the coaches. Guys would hog the ball and try to score a lot of points, and if they passed it at all they only passed it to their buddy, who wasn't going to pass it to you either. Anyway, it was hard to break into the clique. Then there was the Tennessee clique, too.

Nobody knew me and I didn't have anyone watching out for me. It was more like, "Where did this guy come from?" I developed a different kind of strategy to get noticed. Since I knew I wasn't going to get the ball very much, I decided to concentrate on making an impression through my defense and rebounding. Once in a while I got the ball, but I didn't force my shots. I actually passed the ball. This happens a lot in tryout sessions where the players try to impress coaches by doing flashy stuff. I focused on the hard work stuff, the nitty-gritty stuff. Coaches say they like players who do that stuff, but it's just harder to get noticed in tryouts where people aren't playing a team game.

I was flying all around grabbing rebounds, and that worked out for me. They started calling me "The Flying Dutchman" because I was all over the place. We had that basketball camp for about three weeks and then split up and went home for the rest of the summer. There were two weeks more of vacation before school started. But I didn't go back to North Carolina for a couple of reasons. I stayed because I didn't have the money for train fare and I didn't want to go back home and go back to work in the cotton fields, either. I also thought it would be more beneficial for me to stay at Tennessee State and play in the gym every day. I needed the practice. One other guy, Vernon McNeal, from Chicago, stayed around, too, and we worked out every day.

It was during this time that I learned my number one offensive weapon from Vernon: The jump shot! He was a good teacher because he was such a good shooter, even though he was a guard who was only between 5-foot-10 and six feet tall and I was a big man. He was also adept at shooting left- and right-hand hook shots. I was a quick study and added those weapons to my arsenal.

Before college I had never taken a jump shot. The jump shot was a new weapon at that time. Most players still used the set shot for long-range shooting. The taller, inside guys mixed up hooks and short push shots from in the lane. But when I stayed in Nashville to practice I began taking jump shots for the first time in my life. I worked pretty hard on it. I was a good jumper, so I got good elevation. We were the only ones around at the time — no coaches. Later, when the coaches saw me taking jump shots they were surprised.

When regular practice began and the team was broken up for two sides in scrimmages I got to show off my jumper. Tennessee State had a very special college sports program going. The football team was great and won national championships. The basketball team could recruit all of the best players who came to town for the national high school tournament. Schools like the University of Tennessee and Memphis State didn't recruit black players then. Definitely not, especially since they were in the South. You couldn't even have games between white and black players back then. It was against the law in some states.

A lot of the guys who didn't make the basketball team coming out of that summer camp never played anywhere else. They had their chance, didn't make the grade, and they just went home. Some of the other guys hooked on at other schools. Some of them still went to school at Tennessee State and played intramural ball.

After two years we got a new head coach, the famous John McClendon, who had been coaching at North Carolina College when I was in high school. He said he was going to recruit me, but he just got there too late, I guess. I had already gone to Tennessee.

I made the cut from the summer camp and worked hard on my jump shot, but when the season began I was a back-up. I was only a freshman and I didn't start until one of the holdover players got sick. He got a case of hives, or something like that, and I filled in as a starter before the end of my freshman year, the 1951-1952 season. There were only three holdover players from the year before and there were nine or ten freshmen. We were a very good team.

When I enrolled in college my plan was to major in business, but the coaches thought I should major in physical education. The idea was that at least later in life I would be qualified to coach if that was my major.

Coach Cash was probably about 5-foot-4 and he was a no-nonsense guy. He was from Chicago and believed in fundamentally sound basketball. He was not a fast-break guy. He despised it and called it "race horse basketball." He was a technician. He wanted us to play half-court. We were supposed to play under control, play defense and run our offense in the half-court. We had to pass the ball around a lot before taking a shot. It was all strictly fundamental. A lot of us were playing wide-open basketball, running more, so he had to keep a reign on some of us. We loved to run and shoot. That was me. I liked that style.

It wasn't as if I was a gunner because I passed the ball around and I liked to play defense and rebound. I shot once in a while, but I was one of the more liberal guys on the team with the ball. Most of my teammates did not aspire to be great passers. They wanted to shoot. I didn't depend on them giving me the ball all of the time. When I was rebounding at the offensive end I'd get a lot of tip-ins and put-backs for my points. But if I had an open shot from the corner I took that.

I grew up in a small town and I hadn't been anywhere before I went to college, so that made the road trips kind of interesting. It was fun going to new places and it was fun hanging out with my teammates, but it didn't seem like that big a deal to me. It was good to travel, but I was more interested in winning basketball games. I was focused on what we were doing.

During my time with the basketball team we went to a lot of places. I went to Minneapolis and St. Paul, to Ohio, Kentucky, South Dakota, all over the country. And we played exhibitions in Cuba. At that time in the 1950s there was a lot of discrimination in Cuba against darker skinned people. All of the fancy casino areas and the best beaches were reserved for white tourists. We never went to the beach on our road trips. Blacks weren't exactly welcomed. When we went to northern cities in Minnesota or South Dakota and we went out to eat, people were outwardly very friendly.

It didn't matter that we were a black team going to a restaurant in Minneapolis. It was different from North Carolina and Tennessee. They were making money. It wasn't an individual thing where they would turn you away. In the South they accept you individually, but in a group that's where the problem comes in. Most people down there had some black people that they knew individually and were pretty close to. As a group it's different.

George Altman

We won the National Black Basketball Championship my freshman year. We were very good. In high school, when the season ended, I would go on to play baseball in the spring. But Tennessee State did not have a baseball team my freshman year. Didn't have one my sophomore year, either. The team started when I was a junior. Those were two crucial years lost in my baseball development.

After freshman year of basketball, I didn't really miss baseball at first. I didn't give it a thought. I was concentrating on college basketball. I was immersed in basketball. After school got out following my freshman year I went to New York and visited my cousins. I did go to see the Brooklyn Dodgers play. I spent the summer there and then after my sophomore year, when we won the National Black Basketball Championship again, I spent the summer working in Connecticut. I didn't play any baseball.

At that point, I began thinking about the prospect of playing professional basketball. Except for watching games on TV, baseball was out of my life at the time. I was aiming for basketball. At the end of my sophomore year in college there was no way that I would have imagined that I would become a professional baseball player.

My junior year, Coach McLendon replaced Coach Cash as the basketball coach. I am not sure Coach Cash was actually fired, but I think the administration put a lot of pressure on him to quit. Technically, he quit. He didn't really want to. We were a winning team, too, but I don't think the athletic director liked our style. The slower, fundamental game wasn't entertaining enough for him, even though we were winning. Not too many people argue with success. I had pretty good luck with Coach Cash and I liked him, so I was not excited that he was out. I was a little bit disappointed, but we knew that Coach McLendon was coming in. He had such a reputation, that was a bonus.

I was a speedster so I knew the new style would be to my benefit. I had done a lot of running and so had some of our other guys. We had the horses to run, but Coach Cash had the harness on us most of the time.

Things changed a lot with Coach McLendon. We won a Christmas invitational tournament in 1954. There were white teams in that tournament and we got noticed. After that we were invited to Kansas City to play in the NAIA championships. The NAIA had voted to allow historically black schools to play in the tournament, and although the school's greatest achievements came after I graduated, John McClendon's Tennessee State team won three straight titles in 1957, 1958 and 1959.

Coach McClendon did believe in the fast break and he relied on it. He was one of the first coaches to popularize it in college play. He should have ended up in the college and professional basketball Halls of Fame. Coach McClendon liked the way I played. I was always jumping. If I didn't get the ball the first time, I kept rebounding. I jumped and jumped and jumped. Coach McLendon would tell the team, "Do it like George Altman." Years later at an alumni reunion one of the other players told me, "Man, I used to hate you!" You can start breathing hard just from jumping up and down. It's not too friendly on the knees, either.

We didn't have the world's fanciest living quarters. Four of us lived together to save money. We had double bunk beds that we slept on. We all got along. Nobody snored. We didn't have any problems. One thing we all had in common was that we never thought we would go to college at all and now that we were on great basketball teams we were quasi-celebrities around campus. We were big on campus. We got recognized when we were walking around. In the cafeteria it meant that we got a little extra in our servings.

I was really pretty much a novice at basketball when I entered Tennessee State. I had only played two years in high school, so I was still learning the game. After a couple of years, though, I did think I might be good enough to play in the pros. Coach Cash did help me pick up the fundamentals and pattern plays of the game with a lot of picking and cutting.

We played against white schools, but we only played them in the North. We weren't going to be playing against any of the colleges in Georgia or Arkansas. There were never any racial incidents of any kind that I'm aware of that happened while playing the white schools.

Besides those games in Cuba we also played against Army teams. Coach McLendon went after the best competition he could find. Coach McLendon was a low-key guy most of the time, but he was intense. Dick Barnett, who was the star guard on those later championship teams and then had a long career in the NBA, kept a blog and I think he wrote that Coach McLendon had "a quiet fury." He didn't yell at us, but that didn't mean he was a softy.

Right away, the first thing Coach McClendon did was have us run three miles before practice. Everybody pretty much groaned. Then during practice it was running, running, running almost every day. The way he played, you had to be in shape. We had one game against Knoxville College where the final score was something like 125–100. They were a running team and we were a running team. It was run and gun.

One reason some of the guys weren't too happy about running was that some of them smoked cigarettes. A lot of them started realizing that they might have to cut down on desserts, too, if they wanted to be in top shape. I was gung ho about running. Running didn't bother me. I liked it.

Coach McLendon was making sure that we were in shape for his style of basketball and he didn't let up when the season started either. He kept us running. That was one big difference with Coach Cash. The pace of the games was different, too, of course. Some of my teammates got on me about the running because I liked doing it. I was always out front in the runs. They gave me some grief about it. But we all had good stamina. My teammates would say things like, "Slow it down, will you?" That kind of thing. They figured if I ran slower they could all run slower.

Coach McLendon was pretty demanding. He made it clear that he wanted us running all of the time. If we got the rebound off the backboard, we ran. If you were playing pickup ball in the gym, he wanted you to run. That's the way we played. You got the ball and you ran. And that's the way we liked to play. We had a bunch of speedsters and that was the best way for us to win.

Once Coach McLendon was in and recruited his own team with new players, we were all racehorses. He recruited for speed. Coach McLendon believed in conditioning and his fast-break style of play. He knew talent when he saw it and then when he had to be, if we were in a close game, he could be a technician. He had some nice plays, out of bounds plays, half-court plays. Mostly he wanted to put the pressure on other teams by moving, but after that he also believed in discipline in our game. We moved, moved, moved the ball and wore down the other team with our stamina. We had a strong bench. If you were tired, you could sit down for a while.

It was a privilege to play for Coach McLendon. He had a nice, even demeanor. He was confident. He knew his stuff and he would build the guys up a little bit. He'd let you know when you were playing well and that he thought you had good talent. He gave us positive reinforcement. He was not anything like a Leo Durocher, who managed us when I was with the Cubs. Durocher was not the type to offer encouraging words. I think as an athlete I responded better to a coach that would compliment you and encourage you.

I'm a little more intense than most guys. I could be hard on myself. Going back to when I first became involved in competition, I always wanted to be the best. I put a lot of internal pressure on myself to do well and perform. Very rarely did I play relaxed, because I wanted to win so badly. That was true at Tennessee State and later when I played for the Cubs, too. I had won in grade school. I won in high school. I won in college. My team won in the service. When I got to the Cubs I still wanted to win all of the time. As everyone knows, that's not what the Cubs were doing at that time when I was there.

That fire didn't come from my family and certainly not from my father, who didn't pay attention to sports. I wondered where it came from and decided that it was because I was an only child. I had no one to boost me up or look out for me, so there were a lot of times I got into those fights without any help and was picked on. So when I got other guys in a game I figured I could get back at them. This was my way of beating them. I got them back and I got everyone back by winning.

That attitude really did help me out in my sports career at all levels. The type of training we did with Coach McLendon also helped me out later when I was playing in Japan. In Japan they go out of their way to train extra hard. It's hard and you've really got to want to do it and go along with their routines. I had already been through it.

Coach McLendon became the first African American head coach at a white college when he took over at Cleveland State, and he became the first African American head coach of a professional team when he coached the Cleveland Pipers in the American Basketball Association. His Tennessee State teams also won those three NAIA championships in the 1950s. No black school had done that. He was a pioneer in a lot of ways. I believe strongly that Coach McLendon and Buck O'Neil should long ago have been enshrined in the Halls of Fame available to them in their respective sports.

Coach McClendon was enshrined in the Naismith Basketball Hall of Fame in Springfield, Massachusetts, but it was as a contributor, not for coaching. I think being a contributor covered a lot of things, including being one of the proponents of the fast break. But he wasn't elected as a coach and he should be. Dick Barnett has been running a campaign for Coach McLendon to get into the Hall that way. I get emails about it all of the time.

When Coach McLendon came to Tennessee State I had heard of him, but I didn't know his reputation was that great. I guess he was still building it at the time. It's one of those things you realize later. He taught me things that helped me in athletics later on and he certainly trained me to be in the best shape of my life.

He taught me what hard work is in sports. If you are competing in sports you need to be in condition not only physically, but with a winning mindset. He taught us what we needed to do to win. We played against his old team, Hampton Institute, regularly before he came to Tennessee State. I think we came out ahead about four of the times we played them. I think he beat us once or twice.

It happens a lot now because new coaches take over teams after they've been losing, but we weren't worried that Coach McLendon was going to bring in all new guys over us when he arrived. That's because we had a ready-made team that was good. We were the same team that had won all of those games starting when we were freshmen, and most of us were still there. I think Coach McLendon brought one guy with him when he came who was from Michigan, but he didn't crack the lineup.

He adapted us to his style and then when we graduated, Coach McLendon went out and got all new players and won three national titles in a row. So you would have to say he knew what he was doing.

3

Back to Baseball

Given the way his life turned out, anyone who knew George Altman in adulthood would be surprised to hear that he gave up baseball and it was almost a foregone conclusion that he wasn't going to participate in the sport anymore once he set his heart on basketball.

Enjoying great success on the court and playing with a winning hoops team was enough for Altman. He missed baseball a little bit when he thought about it, but he didn't really think much about it.

After two seasons with the Tennessee State basketball team, Altman considered himself as a ripe candidate to make money in the sport as a professional after he graduated from college. He hadn't played baseball in two years, and if two major developments hadn't occurred, it is likely that the world at large would never have heard of George Altman the baseball player.

The first thing that made Altman rethink his sports future was a knee injury suffered on the basketball court his junior year. The second thing — and by far the most important twist that affected his life as he moved into his 20s — was a decision made by the administration of Tennessee State to add a baseball team to the roster of team sports offered to students.

It was not long after resuming his temporarily put-aside baseball career in college that Altman got a chance to play for the legendary Kansas City Monarchs under Buck O'Neil in the waning days of the Negro Leagues.

The president of Tennessee State was a baseball fan and some of the assistant coaches with the football team were baseball players. Officials decided that with the school having such a great athletic program it was a shame that there was no baseball team.

We had a lot of great athletes at the school playing football and basketball. A large number of them had also been baseball players in high school, so we had a lot of guys around with baseball experience. They didn't even really have to go out and recruit a team. We had players right there. It wasn't just football and basketball players on hand, either. There were other guys in the student body who had played baseball and wanted to play again. They had the background and talent.

The school announced that we were going to have a baseball team after the basketball season was over. I definitely wanted to play because I had always loved it. So I showed up for the tryouts, and the ball was still just jumping off the bat. That was pretty good since I had laid off from the sport for two years. I was pretty happy to be playing again. I hadn't missed not playing so much, but once the opportunity was there again I enjoyed it.

During the basketball season I had jammed a knee and it affected my jumping a little bit. It made me wonder about my basketball future. It didn't mean I was going to retire from basketball or miss my senior year, but if there was any long-term impact on my game it would have prevented me from trying to become a professional. I was also a 6-foot-4 forward. That was fine in college at the time, but even in the 1950s that wasn't big enough to be a frontcourt player too many places in the NBA. I would have to make the switch to guard. Now players who are that height are undersized or average guards.

The closest I had come to playing baseball during my layoff was fast-pitch softball once in a while. I'm not sure whether or not that helped me out. Almost everyone on the baseball team that first year was also playing another sport at Tennessee State. When the season began we had two football players and one basketball player in the outfield. A basketball player was the catcher. The shortstop was not on another team, but most of the athletes were from other sports.

There I was playing baseball again and it was great. One of the biggest thrills I had that year was playing exhibition games against some of the Negro Leagues teams that were passing through our area. The heyday of the Negro Leagues had passed. Once Jackie Robinson joined the Brooklyn Dodgers in 1947 and opened the door for other African Americans to play in the majors, Negro Leagues teams began failing. By the mid–1950s only the remnants of the league remained.

The biggest young African American stars, like Hank Aaron, Willie

Mays, and Ernie Banks, were all getting their chances to play in the majors. There was still a team known as the Nashville Stars around, and we played against them. They were semi-professionals and we were still college kids. I think we also played the Birmingham Black Barons.

There were still some big names left on the rosters of those teams. Buck O'Neil was still around. He was the manager of the Kansas City Monarchs right up to the end. Satchel Paige had made it to the majors with the Cleveland Indians and the St. Louis Browns, but after that he continued pitching with any team he could. He went back to the Monarchs, but when I was in college we didn't play against the Monarchs.

We had a very good team. The shortstop was from Mobile, Alabama, and his name was Warren Foster. A lot of great players came out of the Mobile area, including Satchel Paige, Hank Aaron, and Billy Williams. All of those guys are in the Hall of Fame. I think Foster could have gone into baseball, but he went to medical school and became a doctor. We had a player named Leon Jamison who was a natural hitter. Nate Smith was a catcher who signed with the Dodgers. Fred Valentine was a switch-hitting center fielder who had a nice career in the majors and also played in Japan.

Once I started playing again I realized how much I had missed baseball. It was, "Oh, this is great, I really love this." It was as if the sport won me over all over again. The first year they didn't schedule too many games, and then we had a lot of rain that spring and quite a few got called off. So it wasn't a very long season. It was just a fresh taste. It got me excited to play again and to look forward to my senior year.

By my senior year with the Tennessee State basketball team we had been together for four years and knew everyone's habits and moves. We had been playing for John McClendon for a year, so we knew what he expected from us. That team, for the 1954-55 season, was really good. We won almost all of our games. But that year, after winning three straight black national championships, we lost. Texas Southern beat us. We had them by 19 points at the half. What happened was that the main referee in the tournament was a graduate of Tennessee State and he was taking heat that he had given us some home cooking in the past. Then in the championship he went the other way.

We had a couple of guys foul out against Texas Southern that had never fouled out of a game during the season, and that hurt us. One of our top backups, big Marvin Roberts, a great shooter at center, developed a heart problem. He couldn't play more than five or ten minutes at a time. We ended up losing by a basket or one point. Texas Southern had a big star, too. Woody Saulsberry, who had a good career in the NBA, was their top guy. In the pros he averaged double figures and won a championship, so he was the real deal. They had a couple of other guys who played some professional ball or played with the Harlem Globetrotters. They got us in the end. I have to admit that they were pretty good.

After two years of playing basketball I thought I was a prospect to play pro ball. But after four years of playing college basketball I had my doubts. My knees started giving me trouble. They were wearing down from all that jumping. It wasn't a problem in every game. Nothing like that. But when we played in a tournament and we played every day for a few days in a row I could feel it by that second or third game. If you played in the pros, of course, you played many more games than you did in college. It was a much longer season and they had back-to-back games. I didn't know if my body would hold up to that grind.

At the end of the season my game was suffering a little bit. I wasn't drafted by any pro team. My thoughts began shifting to using my college major for a career. I started thinking about coaching again. I had a feeler to see if I was interested in coaching at Lemoyne College in Memphis. But I had one more season of college baseball to play before I worried about what I was going to do with the rest of my life.

I'm not sure what my batting average was in college, but I think I hit about .380 my junior year. I wasn't quite as good as a senior and nobody seemed to be scouting me or approaching me with any type of baseball opportunity. I had a pretty thin resume in the sport at that time. During the last summer I was working in Connecticut and someone told me that the Cleveland Indians had a scout around to look at me, but nothing came of it. I never heard anything again about that. Months went by after that, the whole school year, and I hadn't heard anything, so I didn't think the opportunity was there in baseball.

You know we really had a short schedule. We didn't play that many games, so we didn't get much exposure. It wasn't like today where a scout will find you wherever you are playing, whether it is at an obscure high school or in the Dominican Republic. Someone had to make a connection for you. In my case, as summer came along, J. C. Kincaide, the assistant athletic director at Tennessee State, came up to me and said, "Do you want to play ball? I think you can make it."

I wasn't doing anything at all that summer, so my answer wasn't very hard to figure out. I said, "Sure." He made some telephone calls. I don't even know who he called. But I know he did make contact with the Kansas

George Altman said one of the greatest experiences of his life was playing for the Kansas City Monarchs during the waning days of the Negro Leagues in 1955. This photo was taken much later when he showed off a Monarchs uniform.

City Monarchs. I don't know if was the owner of the team, Buck O'Neil, or someone else. He called them on the phone and said something like, "Hey, I've got a kid you might want to take a look at."

Mr. Kincaide had faith in me. He had seen me play and he felt I was a good athlete and that if I got some more experience I could play professional baseball. Then a lot of things started happening in a short period of time. I graduated on time from Tennessee State with my degree in physical education. But all of a sudden I got an offer to become the basketball coach at Lemoyne. I was only 22, but I had played for some good coaches, so I thought I could do it. It was a four-year school, so it was a lot of responsibility. But I was a fast learner.

I never took that job because the Kansas City Monarchs showed interest in me. After Mr. Kincaide made the phone call they OK'd a tryout for me. The Monarchs were coming to Indianapolis to play some games over a weekend and they asked me to meet them there. Indianapolis is maybe 300 miles from Nashville, but it's a straight shot driving and I went north. I can't even remember how I got there, if I took a train or what, but they probably paid the fare.

I joined up with the Monarchs in Indianapolis and met Buck O'Neil for the first time. O'Neil, who gained late-in-life fame as a storyteller in the widely embraced Ken Burns documentary "Baseball," recognized talent when he saw it and was renowned for teaching young players the nuances of the game.

After I got to Indianapolis I thought the Monarchs were going to ask me to try out over a period of a couple of days and that in between I would sit on their bench and watch them play their games. I took batting practice and when it was over I sat down on the bench, prepared to watch the game and take some more cuts the next day before the next game.

Evidently I must have impressed them a little bit because as I was getting comfortable on the bench, sitting back to just enjoy the game, Buck came up to me and said, "Boy, you're in there." It almost scared me to death.

I didn't even know I had been hired, and there I was in the lineup playing the outfield for the Kansas City Monarchs.

4

The Kansas City Monarchs

Young George Altman could not have found a better place to continue his baseball education than on the Kansas City Monarchs managed by Buck O'Neil. O'Neil was a sharp handler of players, especially inexperienced ones on their way up. He was also the bridge between the old days of the Negro Leagues and the last days of the Negro Leagues as Major League integration slowly strangled what had once been a lifeline for African American players.

By the time Altman completed his degree at Tennessee State in 1955, the end of the Negro Leagues was in sight. Baseball was opening the doors to black players, slowly but steadily, and although it took 12 years until the last team integrated its roster, that process was complete by 1959.

As a player, O'Neil wielded a healthy stick, five times batting more than .300 during a career that spanned 1937 to 1950, with a high of .338. Eventually, O'Neil became player-manager for the Monarchs and then solely manager. As the league gradually fizzled out, O'Neil remained one of the bedrock connecting figures who had known and played with all of the greats of a bygone era.

By the 1950s, O'Neil was playing a dual role, running the storied franchise on the field while also steering young black players to the majors.

The Monarchs themselves were the oldest and longest-running franchise in Negro Leagues baseball. The team was founded in 1920 and participated in the Negro National League until 1931 when that league folded. The Monarchs played on as an independent team between 1932 and 1936 and then joined the Negro American League in 1937, sticking it out until the end in 1961. Even then the Monarchs stayed in business as an independent squad through 1965.

A lot of history was associated with the Monarchs. Owner J. L. Wilkin-

son was the only white owner in the Negro Leagues. He was also a pioneer in using portable lights for night games. In 1924, the Monarchs won the first Negro Leagues World Series. In all, the Monarchs won 13 league championships.

An extraordinary man, late in life O'Neil lobbied for the creation of the Negro Leagues Museum in Kansas City and was renowned as a speaker and raconteur who helped preserve the legacy of the Negro Leagues and the memory of great players among mainstream baseball fans.

George Altman made O'Neil's acquaintance at his batting tryout, and got to know him during a summer's play. More importantly for Altman's career, however, was O'Neil's expanding connections with the majors. O'Neil was acting unofficially as a scout, pinpointing the best young black players. Soon enough he was officially hired as a scout by the Chicago Cubs, and in the early 1960s became the first African American coach in the majors. Long after he gave up the uniform, O'Neil continued scouting. And when he tried to retire he was immediately offered a job scouting the American League for his hometown Kansas City Royals — without having to leave the stadium.

"I've never known anybody with a more positive outlook toward baseball and life," said then–Royals general manager John Schuerholz. "I wanted some of that to rub off on our younger players."[1]

O'Neil was a nurturer of young players — just what Altman needed at the time. For a player whose career had been stymied by baseball's prejudice, O'Neil was also remarkably free of bitterness, and he imparted his attitude to the young black players he tutored who were about to gain the opportunity he had missed out on of being signed by big-league teams.

Buck O'Neil put me in the lineup with the Monarchs and I stayed in the lineup. I don't even remember negotiating a contract. I don't think there was a written contract or anything like that. I might have been paid $300 a month and although that doesn't sound like a lot, it was big money for me just coming out of college and never having had a regular job.

That was great, especially for playing ball, for playing sports. I had just played four years of sports in college for no salary, although I appreciated the immeasurable benefits of a college education. It was somewhat surprising that after I had given up on baseball and taken time off from baseball that I was now playing baseball professionally.

My whole thinking process changed all over again. It reverted back to the thoughts I had in mind when I was a kid and listening to baseball games on the radio. Back then I was thinking, "Hey, given the opportunity, maybe I can make it as a professional player." I envisioned myself like Stan Musial hitting. 340 and driving in 100 runs. That sort of thing.

I started thinking about what I might be able to accomplish in baseball, and the Monarchs gave me the opportunity to play every day. I was very appreciative, especially playing under the guidance of a guy like Buck O'Neil. He was an encourager. If you struck out he would say something like, "It's alright. It's OK. You'll get 'em next time." When you were up at the plate you could hear him from the bench going, "Light 'em up, boy! Come on, you can do it. You're better than he is."

That's what I liked about Buck. He was not only a teacher, but an encourager. I knew he had seen a lot of talent and if he thought highly of me then it meant I must have something. So that was very inspirational.

When I was growing up in Goldsboro and going to college in Nashville I did not know much about the Kansas City Monarchs or the Negro Leagues. My personal knowledge was when a team came through Nashville and played a game. What I read about the Monarchs was that they had been the team of Jackie Robinson and Ernie Banks. When I read that history, that's what really impressed me about the organization.

I joined the Monarchs after I graduated, so it was near the end of June. It was also near the end of the Negro American League as a formal league keeping statistics and standings instead of just being a group of teams that played exhibitions and toured. By 1955 most everything was on the road barnstorming. I remember one time we were in Chicago for the All-Star Game at Comiskey Park and right after the game we got on the bus because we had a game the next night in Columbus, Mississippi. That was a long haul.

Another time when we were in Chicago we got to go to Wrigley Field as a team. It was the day that Ernie Banks either tied or broke the single-season record for grand slam home runs. We were so proud that a former Monarch was setting records in the majors. At the time I had no idea that one day I would be batting behind such a superstar.

We went everywhere by bus and we did a lot of sleeping on the bus. You would ride long distances and then play a game right away. I'll tell

George Altman enjoying a display at the Negro Leagues Museum in Kansas City.

you, traveling through the South in the summer with the heat and humidity and wearing wool uniforms, your outfits took a beating. A lot of times after we finished a game we got right back on the bus. Our uniforms were all sweaty and we didn't have a chance to dry them or wash them. We didn't always get to the laundry.

In the major leagues, you go home at night and come back the next day and you have fresh uniforms. In our situation we had to pack up our wet uniforms. We tried to get to the ballpark for our next game early enough to air them out. But some days we just didn't get there in time and when we took the uniforms out, phew! They were pretty uncomfortable to put back on in that condition, too. Thank goodness those days were very rare.

Going by bus for hundreds of miles at a time was not the optimum way to get rest. I was a good sleeper on buses, so it didn't bother me too much, but a lot of times the bus was pretty noisy. You had a whole team and guys were talking and playing cards. There was a lot of carrying on. It was a group of guys trying to have fun. There were plenty of times we started games where we were pretty tired.

This was also the mid–1950s, so travel through the South presented its own problems. There were plenty of places we couldn't stay and there were plenty of places we couldn't eat. A lot of the time when we got to a town we stayed in private homes in the black community or in black-owned bed and breakfasts. Those were destinations. By that I mean we didn't stop at night on the way someplace. We drove through the night to reach a place where we knew we would be welcome.

There were times you drove all night long and drove right up to the ballpark for a scheduled game. You might have time to get those uniforms unpacked and cleaned up some, or you might not. Then we might go to a place we had picked out to stay after the game. The manager knew where we were going, but we didn't.

Most of the baseball greats who played in the Negro Leagues were gone by the time I played. Players like Josh Gibson, who died young, Cool Papa Bell, and others who never played in the majors. They were too old when integration started. Satchel Paige was still playing, though. He had been a legend for a long time and did play in the majors when he was in his early 40s. Now he was getting to be in his late 40s, although nobody knew what his actual age was.

That summer of 1955 Satchel came back and rejoined the Monarchs. He was either 47 or 49, depending on who you believe. I knew of his reputation as a legendary pitcher, and he came to us without any spring training. I think he had retired and was coming out of retirement. He really wasn't in shape when he showed up. I'm not sure he ever went to spring training with any team. I think he just hired himself out to local teams and kept moving from team to team. From everything I ever heard about him, Satchel was not one for serious training as we know it. He just kept going from place to place pitching. He believed in pitching himself into top form.

I'm not 100 percent sure that Satchel knew all of our names. He called us "Young Bloods." He definitely called me "Young Blood." We didn't talk to him that much because he didn't travel with us most of the time. He had his own Cadillac and he followed the bus. Sometimes he showed up late to the park. He was his own man.

Satchel joined us in Birmingham and he hadn't had any training or anything. I think there was supposed to be some kind of agreement that the other team would take it easy on Satchel. He was the big draw. So guys generally took it easy on Satchel. But the young guys on the other team, evidently they didn't get the word, or if they got the word they didn't pay any attention. They started hitting him all over the place. Satch came back to the dugout and said, "That's okay. Wait till I see them the next time. Next time I see them things will be different." Sure enough, two or three weeks later we played Birmingham again and Satchel pitched. He set them down, three up, three down, for three innings.

He still had that control and he was in better shape. He wasn't as fast as he used to be, but he had the control. He could knock you down and throw the next pea on the outside corner. That kind of thing. He might have been almost 50 years old, but he was still impressive to watch. He also fashioned himself to be a hitter and he hit a few line drives in some clutch situations. He wasn't a great hitter, but he could make contact. He wasn't as good a hitter as he said he was, but he had confidence and could talk himself into producing.

Satchel was a showman. He did a lot of talking to the hitters. It was rumored that he and Josh Gibson did a lot of bantering when they faced each other on the diamond. That seemed to be in line with what I saw from him. Again, I think it was a game against Birmingham and one of the young guys was mouthing off at him. When the kid was coming up to bat, Satchel walked up near him and said, "Alright, young man, young blood, tell me what kind of pitches you like to miss?" Then he proceeded to strike him out on three pitches. The guy knew what pitches were coming and still Satchel struck him out. Those were the kind of stories I heard and saw with Satchel. There were those stories that when he was younger he would wave the outfield in and then strike out the side. He didn't do that when I was around him, though. That was in his young days.

One thing I did notice was that at that point Satchel seemed to have a digestive problem. He was burping a lot. Remember he had those rules for living good and one of them was not to "angry up the blood by eating fried foods." I guess that was real. He definitely had stomach miseries.

Satchel was entertaining to be around, but Buck O'Neil was my

38

first real mentor. He was 55 years old and he was still playing some. I had been an outfielder all of the way, but Buck taught me how to play first base and I played first base for the Monarchs that summer. He taught me all the moves around the bag when receiving the throws from the infielders. As far as Buck playing goes, I remember the last time he played the field. We were playing a game in Lexington, Kentucky, and that's where we picked up Lou Johnson, who later played in the majors.

Buck decided to play third base that day, and the quality of the field wasn't so good. On the mound was Enrique Moroto. He was a temperamental Cuban pitcher, but he had a good fastball and curve. He got upset, though, if someone made an error behind him. He would pout on the mound and end up not concentrating and not throwing his best stuff. Sure enough someone made an error and over at third base Buck could tell he was upset, and Buck thought he was just goosing the ball up there.

Right after that someone on the other team hit a shot down the third-base line at Buck. The ball hit off his leg and his shin. Buck could hardly walk. He hobbled out to the mound — and he had that big voice he was known for — and you could hear him all over the stadium. He said, "Boy, if you don't get something on the ball, you and I are going to go round and round right here on the mound!"

Buck didn't want to have any more line drives hit at him. After that you could hear that catcher's mitt popping. Moroto was throwing aspirin tablets up there. But that was the last time Buck played the field.

Before games, as the manager, Buck would watch you in batting practice and talk about the pitcher you were going to face. He would say things like the guy was going to throw inside or something like that. He was familiar with the pitchers and he would tell you what to expect. The guy was going to throw curves in a certain situation and you were better off trying to pull the ball to left. Those are the kind of tips he would give you. He'd watch you take some swings and let you know if your stance was off, if you were stepping in the bucket.

During my time with the Monarchs I also heard stories about the great ballplayers that had come before me in the Negro Leagues who were either retired or had died. Of course some of those stories were exaggerated. I heard the one about Cool Papa Bell. Everyone said how fast he was and the story went, "Cool Papa's so fast he hit a ball up the middle and the ball hit him in the rear end as he was sliding into second base." Cool Papa Bell got faster every year after he retired.

To me it is a shame that Buck O'Neil is not in the Baseball Hall of Fame. There is no doubt that he should be in there. Not only was he a great ballplayer, but he was also a scout, a super-scout, one of the greatest managers I know of and an ambassador for baseball. I don't think anybody I can think of did more for baseball, and especially for the Negro Leagues, than Buck O'Neil. He was a walking history book.

In 2006, when they had the vote that re-examined the records of players from the Negro Leagues from the past and they took 17 people in, I don't see how he got left out. There was no way he should have been left out. I think they recognized a mistake was made when the Hall of Fame put up a statue of him and created the Buck O'Neil Award to honor him.

Buck ran many championship teams and he played at the same time. He was instrumental in getting a lot of those players into the Hall of Fame by accelerating their careers. He was also a very eloquent spokesman for the Negro Leagues. He educated everybody.

I only played for the Kansas City Monarchs in June, July and August of 1955, for about three months. At the end of the season I didn't know that league play was coming to an end, so I was able to think that I might be able to play again the following summer. I didn't know what the future of the Monarchs was. I was lucky I got to do it and be part of the Negro Leagues because that year was pretty much the end of the league as we knew it. After that it was pretty much all barnstorming for the Monarchs.

When the season ended, so did my affiliation with the Monarchs, although I never forgot that cherished experience. When September came around I went back to school at Tennessee State. I was starting work on a masters degree in case I ever wanted to work in athletic administration. I also helped out with the basketball team as an assistant coach while I was going to class.

Although I was serious about earning another degree at Tennessee State — even after I had been paid to play baseball — that plan lasted only one semester. I may have been finished with the Monarchs, but I was not done with professional baseball. It turns out I was just starting.

5

The Minors, the Army
and Making the Cubs

Although George Altman played just one summer for the storied Kansas City Monarchs, his relationship with and links to Buck O'Neil proved to be timely and life-altering. As the Negro American League wound down, O'Neil had to make a choice between staying with his beloved Monarchs as the team devolved into a barnstorming club, or take advantage of the only avenue open to him in organized baseball.

In his mid-fifties, O'Neil was too old to play in the majors. That ship had sailed. No team was going to hire him directly from the Monarchs to manage or coach in the big leagues. The Chicago Cubs approached him with the offer of becoming a scout. Recognizing that the untapped market of African American players was now here to stay, O'Neil's specialty was to act as a link between the Cubs and unknown (to them) black talent.

O'Neil had already established ties to the Cubs. He sent the team Ernie Banks, arguably the greatest star in the history of the team and the player who came to be known as "Mr. Cub" as he played 19 seasons for the franchise and earned his way into the Hall of Fame.

Altman did not have the same credentials as Banks, but he benefited from his tie-in with O'Neil. O'Neil not only vouched for him as a player with the type of talent who could make it to the big club, he was instrumental in Altman signing with the Cubs.

For one semester after playing with the Monarchs, Altman worked on his master's degree back at Tennessee State. But the offer from the Cubs was too sweet to pass up. Not financially, because there was no huge windfall, but for the opportunity. Altman was making the leap from the all-black Kansas City Monarchs to a big-league club.

In 1959, he surprised everyone with how well he played in spring train-
ing at Mesa, Arizona. "If he keeps on going at this pace, I don't see how we
can keep him out of the starting lineup," Scheffing said in Arizona. Scheffing
didn't and at the end of spring training Altman was awarded a $150 watch
emblematic of the Cubs' best rookie in spring training.[2]

It was all because of Buck O'Neil. The Cubs signed me, Lou Johnson, and J. C. Hartman all together on Buck's say-so. All three of us
signed as amateur free agents before the end of 1955 and the Cubs paid
Kansas City something like $11,000. Then in March of 1956 we were sent
to spring training in Lafayette, Louisiana. This was the minor league
training camp.

The Cubs were not spending a lot of money on prospects like me
at the time. I tell people that my signing bonus was a pack of gum from
the Wrigley family. When I started to play I was probably making about
the same amount of money I got for playing with the Monarchs, about
$300 a month.

The Cubs looked at all three of us in that camp and then decided
where to send us. I was sent to Burlington, Iowa, to play Class B ball.
Lou Johnson and Hartman were sent to Ponca City, Oklahoma. We were
in one of two minor league camps the Cubs had that year. We were players being considered for the low minors. I had a pretty good spring evidently because I was sent to Class B. Class B was the highest level you
could go to from that camp. The AAA and AA guys were in another
camp. So I made a good impression.

We all pretty much made Buck O'Neil look smart — eventually. All
three of us made the majors. J. C. Hartman played parts of two seasons
with the Houston Colt .45s before they became the Astros, starting in
1962. He was 28 when he was a rookie and he got into 51 games. He only
batted .223, though. The next year he got into just 39 games and hit only
.122. That was the end of his major league career, but he did make it to
The Show.

Lou Johnson did better. It took until 1960 for him to make the Cubs
roster and he played just that one year in Chicago. But Lou stayed in the
majors for eight years, mostly with the Los Angeles Dodgers. He had
some good seasons with them. Lou's lifetime average was .258 and in
1966 he had a really good year. Lou hit 17 home runs with 73 RBI and

played in 152 games. Although it wasn't his absolute best season, Lou also had a good year in 1965 and had the good fortune to play in 131 games that season when the Dodgers won the World Series. Lou has a great personality and he became very popular in Los Angeles where he became known as "Sweet Lou" Johnson.

Burlington was in the Three-I League, and even though Iowa was a northern state in the Midwest there were a lot of derisive comments made towards black players. Some teams had players who would call you "shine" and that kind of stuff. Players and their fans for some of the teams — and some of those teams were still all-white in 1956.

At that time Quincy, Illinois, was the worst place in the league. That's where a lot of those derisive comments were made. They didn't have any black players. I think they had one Hawaiian player and that was about it. Even if those minor-league teams had black players they seemed to have a quota, one or two, but never any more than that. Of course if they had two black players they roomed together. I can't say I was surprised to have insults thrown out. I was still thinking of Jackie Robinson breaking in with the Dodgers and all that he went through, so I couldn't consider it to be a surprise.

Nine years had passed since Jackie Robinson went into the majors, but the world hadn't changed that much. When anyone yelled things out I tried to ignore it. I didn't fight back or anything. I figured the best thing to do was ignore it all because you can't win. You're on the road and the crowd isn't going to be on your side.

Burlington had one other African American player at the time. Sam Drake, the infielder, was with me. He also made it to the majors briefly, but not until 1960 with the Cubs, and he played only a few years. But he had a brother, Solly, who was a good player, too. Solly reached the big leagues in 1956 for the first time and then he was out of the majors for a couple of years. Sammy and Solly were the first African American brothers to play in the big leagues.

Sammy was there with me in Burlington for a little while. Then another kid, Doc Connors, came through. He was a good fielding short-stop. But most of the time I was the only African American on the team that summer. Most of the time that meant that the insults fans and players yelled had to be aimed at me. I never even brought it up to management or the team, though. I just kind of lived with it. I tried not

43

to let it get to me and make me so angry that I couldn't focus or concentrate. To succeed, I felt that keeping my focus was the most important thing.

At that time there were a lot of black players showing up around the minors in lots of leagues and a lot of cities that were in the South. The Sally League was notorious for comments made to black players. That's where Hank Aaron came up. In the middle of the 1950s that was something you expected when you signed with a major league team and were headed to the minors. A lot of minor leaguers were going through that kind of thing. It was something that you more or less expected depending on where you were going. I probably didn't expect to hear stuff in Burlington, Iowa, though. I guess we were all kind of reliving the Jackie Robinson story.

We had a lot of Southerners on the ball club, too, and I wasn't all that comfortable with them. They did not insult me like fans in other cities, but it was a subtle kind of treatment. I wasn't close to any of them. For the most part they didn't go out of their way to make me feel completely welcome. However, there was one guy on the team, our right-fielder, who was a nice guy. As a matter of fact, he invited me over to his house for dinner, which was highly unusual. This guy had me over for a meal with him and his wife at their home in Burlington. Other than that I had no contact with any of the guys, except at the ballpark.

That season I lived with a local African American family, a postman and his wife. Sammy Drake lived with another family. I think the team made it known to us that the option of residing with families was available if we wanted to use it. It wasn't as if I had a tough time in town away from the park, but I didn't go out much and socialize much. You kind of kept to yourself. That year I did a lot of reading and the family had a record player. I enjoyed listening to a lot of music and I also started collecting records.

One of my favorites was Dinah Washington. I also liked June Christy and Dakota Staton. I enjoyed jazz. I listened to some Miles Davis stuff and Louis Prima and a guy named King Pleasure.

On the field I thought I did fairly well, so-so really, compared to my expectations. With me a lot of the time it's a matter of adjusting or getting used to new surroundings where I can be comfortable. I played in 120 games and I hit 16 home runs and batted .263. When the season ended nobody from the Cubs really evaluated me or told me how they thought I had done. They didn't say anything like, "We want you to move up next year." I didn't have a lot of time to wonder about it, either, because almost immediately I received a draft notice from the U.S. Army.

I pretty much went straight from Burlington into the Army and was sent to Fort Carson, Colorado. I had never been there and practically had never heard of it, so it was new territory for me. I was not enthusiastic about being drafted. I was already 23 and in Class B baseball. I was way behind the players who started playing pro at 18 or 19 right out of high school. I was already late to the party and now I would have to wait for two more years to resume my baseball career, I thought.

At least there was no war going on at the time. The Korean War had ended and the Vietnam War had not started. I had had some ROTC training in college so I was able to go into the service as a specialist first class. That's like one notch above being a buck private. I went through basic training and while I was waiting to move on from there I played some regimental basketball and was the big gun on the team. We won the regimental basketball championship.

But as part of the training we had to do a two-week off-base stay in the mountains in frigid weather. This was more serious training. We had to bivouac and when I was on that truck I was hating it because I had already been out there for training once with live ammunition and stuff like that. We were crawling down rocky terrain and there were rumors that there were rattlesnakes out there. At the last minute they pulled me off that truck and said I was going to practice with the base basketball team. What a relief! So there I was back to playing basketball for the first time in a couple of years. I liked that a lot more than trying to avoid snakes.

Playing basketball led to playing baseball for the base team. We were really good. We won the All-Army Championship. By then I had already played baseball growing up, in high school, in college, for the Monarchs in the Negro Leagues and a year of minor league baseball. Every area I could, it seemed.

Fort Carson had a monster team. Besides me, we had J. C. Hartman, who had been with the Monarchs, Bobby Ruck, who played AAA, Willie Kirkland, who played with the San Francisco Giants, and a third baseman named Eddie Kopacz, who played in the Giants organization. One of our pitchers was Charley Pride. Charley played in the Negro Leagues and might have become a major leaguer if he hadn't hurt his arm. He was good. Of course, Charley found a new career and became famous as a country and western singer.

By then Charley was a knuckleball pitcher. He was trying to save his career and adjusting to the fact that he couldn't throw as fast anymore. While he was in the Army Charley would perform at the officer's club. And that was really unheard of for a black guy. He was like the black Elvis Presley. One thing about Charley was that you couldn't embarrass him. The guys got on him all of the time for being a hillbilly. It just rolled right off his back.

We also had Ace Robinson as one of our starters. He played with the Memphis Red Sox in the Negro Leagues. He was a hard-throwing left-hander. Ace once tried to pitch games of a doubleheader with Memphis as an iron man act, but only lasted into the second inning of the second game.

And one of our best hitters was Leon Wagner, who had the great nickname of "Daddy Wags." He was coming off a huge year with a lot of home runs in the Carolina League. Charley and Leon used to banter back and forth all of the time about who was the best player between them. Charley used to say that he had a better knuckleball than Hoyt Wilhelm, who got to the Hall of Fame using it. But Charley didn't use his knuckler all of the time, and when he threw a fastball to Leon in batting practice Leon hit him. That fastball was gone. I can tell you when he was young and in his prime it didn't matter if you were throwing a fastball 95 mph or 100 mph, Wagner could wrap your fastball around the right-field flag pole. His hands were so quick.

Leon and Willie Kirkland had some good years in the majors, but I actually thought they would be bigger and do even better than they did. Kirkland was a world beater in the Army. I thought he was going to be a superstar. Daddy Wags played 12 years in the majors, hit more than 30 home runs twice and drove in more than 100 runs twice. Willie played nine years in the big leagues and the most he hit was 27 home runs in a season. He went to Japan afterwards, though, and he hit some home runs over there. But he never lived up to his potential.

They had the ten-run slaughter rule, or mercy rule, as they call it now. Our games hardly ever went past four or five innings. We were just creaming people. We were too good for everybody and that year, 1957, we won the All-Army Championship.

After the baseball season ended, I went back to playing for Fort Carson's basketball team. But I mustered out of the Army before the second baseball season came around in 1958. I had played two years of basketball, but only one year of baseball. Everything would have been different that year anyway. After we won the All-Army Championship we were given a reward of a furlough. All of us went at once and the post commander got pretty upset. So they broke up the team. Everyone else was shipped out except me. They kept me to play on the basketball team. I guess the commander thought we had it too easy.

I was discharged from the Army in 1958, but it was after spring training had ended. The Cubs had me report to Pueblo, a Class A team in Colorado. That was convenient. In fact while I was in the Army I sometimes went to their games. They were right down the road, 40 miles from Fort Carson.

I was already 25 and that was pretty old for a minor leaguer in Class A, but I didn't dwell on that because of my experience playing in the service. I had just been playing with guys who had been in AAA and AA and I held my own. Performing as well as I did in the Army gave my confidence a big boost. When I went to A ball I was right at home. I had a great season for them, batting .325. Actually it was a half season. I played in 89 games.

Once again when the season ended I didn't hear anything from the Cubs. In fact, I stayed right there in Colorado and worked construction. Then I got a lucky offer. After a couple of weeks of doing some work, carrying things up and down ladders, I got the opportunity to play winter ball in Panama. After a couple of weeks of that heavy lifting, I was ready to go back to baseball.

The offer was to play in Panama City. I didn't speak Spanish, but everybody in the Canal Zone spoke English, so it wasn't hard to adjust. It did rain a lot, every day it seemed. They had a big ballpark and the grass always seemed to be wet, either from the rain, or mildew from the dampness.

The players were very nice. Most of the Panamanian players liked to have a good time. After practice they went to bars and drank beer. You could say they weren't training super hard. They were good-time players. There were other American players there and other Hispanic players from the majors or from the high minors. Hector Lopez, the New York Yankees outfielder, was there. Of course, he was from Panama. Also Pancho Herrera played down there. He was from Cuba and played a few years for the Philadelphia Phillies right after that winter.

Another guy on our team was named Alonzo Braithwaite. We nicknamed him "Jackie Robinson," though, because he was such a big Jackie Robinson fan and he talked about him all the time.

The local Panamanian players went to the bars all of the time, but I didn't go out drinking beer with them. I really went to play winter ball to improve. I had a late start in the sport and missed those years being in the Army. Every time I played at a new level and did well it gave me more confidence and experience, and I kept on getting better. Confidence is a huge part of baseball, being relaxed and confident when you play.

All of these things, playing for the Monarchs, playing in the service, playing in Panama, paid off for me. In the spring of 1959 the Cubs sent me to AAA in Houston. That put me one step away from the majors. I was 26 years old and this was going to be a critical season for me. A lot of guys make it to AAA, but never make it to the majors. They stall out and never appear in a major league game. This was a big chance for me, but it came with some pressure.

The contract I signed was to play in Houston. When I got back from Panama, where I hit .280 or .290 with a few home runs, I delivered my car to Houston and went to spring training with the Cubs in Mesa, Arizona. They invited me there, but it didn't seem they wanted me to do much. I was a ball shagger in the outfield a lot of the time like the rest of the young minor-league players in camp. I was earmarked for Houston. I had a AAA contract.

One day at spring training me and a few other guys they had just sprinkled around the field to pick up the balls the regulars hit during batting practice got a break while the team was assembling for the annual team picture. While they were busy taking pictures, the BP pitcher was still on the mound doing nothing. I walked past the batting cage and I grabbed a bat and I yelled, "Come on, throw me some pitches." I just wanted to practice. So he started throwing and I started hitting, and with that thin air in Tucson and being in good shape already from winter ball, the ball was just flying out of the park.

I was hitting the ball over the fence and line drives off the wall. The players taking pictures started making noise about my hitting, going "Woo-hoo" every time I slugged one, and they started teasing some of the other players, mainly Chuck Tanner, saying this rookie was going to take his job. I always could hit in batting practice and I hit really well that day. After I stopped hitting manager, Bob Scheffing sidled up to me and said, "Come down early tomorrow and work out with the big club." From then on I started working out with the Cubs and I got to play in some exhibition games.

That batting practice got me noticed and it gave me a chance. I had a really good spring training. I got really excited. This was beyond my expectations. I was like the other ball shaggers, scheduled to go to the minors. Once I started to work out with the Cubs and play in games, I definitely got the sense that I was in the mix and had a chance to stick.

After a while I even stopped worrying about being sent back. I was being successful at everything I did. I had no reason to worry, but I had no reason before that to think I would stay with the Cubs. But the Army experience was huge because of the way I played with other guys who I knew were ahead of me in the minors, or in the majors. We played against some major league players in the All-Army Championships tournament, such as Bill White and Jackie Brandt. It was just a matter of me getting a chance then. I could always catch the ball and I could hit and run. What else is there?

The only time I thought I might have a problem was when Bob Scheffing came up to me and asked, "Can you play center field?" I said, "Yeah, sure." But I had never played center field except in grammar school. Of course, if you are in a situation like that you are going to say you can handle it. I was always pretty fast and that meant I could cover a lot of ground in the outfield.

Around that time Ty Cobb, who is probably the greatest hitter of all time, came out to camp, and so did Ted Williams. After I played in a few exhibition games there were some articles in the paper about me. Ty Cobb said I looked pretty good. And so did Ted Williams. I read those clippings in the Arizona newspapers and that made me feel pretty darned good. These were a couple of the greatest ballplayers of all time. I knew I was definitely on the right track if those guys were talking about me.

And you know what? The Cubs did trade Chuck Tanner, who later became a great manager. I did take his job. I kind of knew I was going to make the roster because I had been playing center field every day. The Cubs tore up my AAA contract and wrote me a new contract for the Cubs. It's not as if rookies were getting rich at the time, though. My first salary was for something like $5,000 or $6,000 a year.

I was a member of the Chicago Cubs and I was a major league baseball player. It was pretty amazing given my journey after giving up baseball altogether for two years in college. My professional athletic ambitions were being realized, but in a different sport from what I ever expected to find myself playing.

6

The Major Leagues

George Altman was not the youngest of rookies. He made his Major League debut with the Chicago Cubs on April 11, 1959 at age 26, a college graduate, a veteran of the Negro Leagues, and a U.S. Army veteran as well. And now he was an outfielder in the National League.

Altman played center field and right field for the Cubs that year, appearing in 135 of the scheduled 154 games in the pre-expansion era. He smacked 12 home runs and drove in 47 runs that year with a .245 batting average. He also scored 54 runs.

In those days the Cubs were one of the bottom feeders of the National League, and they finished with a record of 74–80. Bob Scheffing was the manager and while Wrigley Field was the home park, it was not quite the tourist attraction it would become. The Cubs draw three million fans a year now, but in 1959 attendance was 858,255, just sixth best in the league.

Among Altman's teammates were Ernie Banks, who won his second consecutive Most Valuable Player Award, young Billy Williams, another future Hall of Famer discovered by Buck O'Neil, and Bobby Thomson, who with the Giants eight years earlier had smashed the home run called "the shot heard around the world" because it was the pennant-winning hit that disposed of the Brooklyn Dodgers.

It was a team short on depth and long on age, but it afforded Altman a chance to play every day as a rookie. He surprised everyone with his readiness in the spring of 1959.

One of the springtime observers credited with having a keen baseball eye was the legendary Ty Cobb, the Hall of Famer who spent most of his career with the Detroit Tigers and who owns the highest lifetime batting average of .357. Cobb liked what he saw of Altman at the plate, including

51

his ability to hit to all fields, to wisely judge the strike zone, and to flash occasional power.

It was Ernie Banks' team. Ernie was a superstar. I had read so much about him. I was amazed at how great he was. He was hitting 40 home runs a year then. Ernie had also played with the Monarchs under Buck, and Buck led him to the Cubs.

Ernie and I lived in the same neighborhood in Chicago and we used to ride to the ballpark together. Ernie drove most of the time, but I did sometimes. He was the big star and maybe he was driving me in order to help out the rookie. We had a good relationship.

Ernie Banks was known as Mr. Cub. He was the face of the team. He was enthusiastic every day, just like you have heard. He had that phrase of his, "Let's play two!" about wanting to play doubleheaders every day, and he was really like that. He would say that every day. A lot of it was for publicity. He had a little poem for every season.

We rode to the park every day, and Ernie didn't really give me many tips about life in the majors, but sometimes he would point things out. For that year, he would say like, "The Cubs are gonna shine in '59." He always had something to say before the season. Like "We're gonna be thrifty in 1960." Or "We're gonna stay alive in '65." He did that for the public, for the newspapers every year, saying how great the Cubs were gonna be. But inside, he really knew that we were not a good team. To us, some of the other players, he might confide and say, "Man, these guys can't play ball." It was bluster when he made those predictions, then I guess reality set in.

Everybody expected him to say it every year. He had to come up with a rhyme. But he knew the team wasn't going to be very good and in those days, for a period of years, the Cubs weren't very good.

I was in awe of the players, especially Ernie Banks. He was one of the guys I idolized. He's an amazing guy the way he took that nice, easy swing and hit the ball right out of there. One thing about Ernie, he had so much natural ability that he didn't have to practice as much as most people. He just had a lot of natural talent.[3]

It's interesting how big a role Buck O'Neil played in sending the Cubs good ballplayers, though. Ernie Banks, Billy Williams and I were all directed to the team by Buck, although Billy didn't play for the Monarchs. Even if the Cubs weren't a pennant-contending team then, the team was much better because of Buck. Buck was a scout when I was a rookie and I didn't see him much at all that year. He didn't join the big club until later as a coach. He wasn't in uniform with the Cubs until 1962.

I first met Billy Williams in A ball, but he was homesick for Mobile, Alabama. He left the Cubs' minor league team and went home. The team sent Buck to go get him and talk him into returning. Buck was a scout and a consultant of some kind. In this case he played the role of a go-between and he patiently talked Billy into continuing in the game.

I actually met my first wife, Rachel, in Pueblo, Colorado, when I was playing there. Buck didn't scout her, though. I had been staying in

Old friends. Visiting with Billy Williams (right) at Wrigley Field, Altman was a businessman in his 40s while Hall of Famer Williams was working with the Cubs as a coach.

a private home with a family and so was Billy. But it got a little bit crowded there and I decided to move out. I moved in with another family, and Rachel was a friend of that family. That's how we met, over at their house.

Although I didn't formally meet her until I was living at that house, I had actually seen Rachel earlier in town when I first got to Pueblo. I was staying in the hotel and she was arguing with someone. It got my attention and I thought, "Wow, that's a beautiful girl." I had no idea I would meet her later and she would become my wife. I was just looking out the window. When I met her at the house I invited her to come to the ballpark and she did. I guess she was a bit of a baseball fan.

We got married in Pueblo in March of 1959, just before I made it with the Cubs. We were married for 13 years. We had two kids together, my son George Altman Jr. and daughter Laura. George graduated from high school in Chicago and went to Triton College for two years. And then he went to Eastern New Mexico in Roswell, New Mexico, to play football. He was a wide receiver and a running back. He also played softball. He was a home-run slugger. After he finished school he stayed in New Mexico, and one night when he was returning from a game, a drunken driver crossed the center line and hit his car and he was killed. George was 25 at the time.

George played softball after he got out of school and was finished with football. He was one of those muscular guys and he had some ridiculous numbers in softball. I had been trying to steer him towards baseball, hopeful that some of that success would carry over from softball. Laura was the oldest child. She was born in 1960. George was born in 1963. Laura lives in Chicago and manages the office of a real estate company that specializes in rehabilitating structures.

So 1959 was a big year. I got married and I made the majors. My first game for the Cubs was against the Los Angeles Dodgers, and they started Don Drysdale. Don Drysdale won a lot of games (209) and he could be very mean on the mound. He was one of those pitchers who wanted to let you know who was boss. It was actually not a good day for baseball. It was cold and rainy and the wind was blowing.

I was definitely nervous before the game. It's hard to believe that anyone wouldn't be somewhat nervous going into their first big-league game. It doesn't matter who you are. It's the top level of baseball. Stan

Musial said he had butterflies before every game. I don't care how long you play, you stay a little bit nervous. I knew I was going to be in the lineup. It wasn't a surprise, but I don't remember being so nervous I couldn't sleep the night before. I had been starting in spring training in all of the exhibition games, but this one counted.

Don Drysdale was known for throwing his fastball inside and high to keep batters off the plate. He also had a reputation of being hard on rookies. He wanted to show you who was in charge right away. My first at-bat — I was batting second in the order that day — he threw a pitch, I think it was an inside slider, on my second or third pitch, that hit me in the right thigh. I don't know if he hit me on purpose, but I would say he was trying to intimidate me. Maybe the ball got a little bit further inside than he wanted it to. It's not as if he apologized for hitting me. He didn't mind hitting me at all.

I didn't get a hit my first time up, but it was better than how I did my first game in the minors. I think I struck out my first three or four times in a row. There was a hard-throwing left-hander and the lights for the night game weren't that good. Against the Dodgers, at least I was on base. And I did get a hit my next time up in that game. In fact, I went two-for-three and I scored a run. That was much better than how I started in the minors. We won the game, 6–1.

The thing I really couldn't believe about the day was that it snowed part of the time. Snowflakes on opening day! I got snowflakes and Don Drysdale to start my career, but we won the game anyway. I don't have the distinct memory of doing it, but I think that night I might have thought, "I'm a major leaguer now." Most players remember their first games, but I sometimes have a tendency to forget some of my big accomplishments. I remember scoring 25 or 28 points in a college game, but I can't remember who we were playing.

I do remember my first home run. I got it on April 29. The Cubs lost to the Cincinnati Reds, 18–8, the night I hit it. Brooks Lawrence was pitching for the Reds. I hit the home run in the sixth inning. It was a two-run homer, but in a game like that you can't make up the difference in runs. Moe Drabowsky started for us and he got the loss. I hit the home run to right field at Crosley Field. They had an elevated right field. Of course, the Reds have played in two ballparks since then. The Cubs are still in Wrigley Field. Wrigley Field, along with Fenway Park, is the oldest park in baseball. It's not just the park, though, some days I'm not sure the Cubs have come into the 21st century, the modern era.

When I was playing, the Cubs had these low-cut socks where the stirrups barely came up over your ankle. Most of the other teams had high-cut socks. Guys used to get on us all of the time about our socks. They called them "ankle breakers." It was a small thing that doesn't seem like much, but we didn't need the distraction.

I liked playing in Wrigley Field, though it wasn't necessarily a hitter's park. It seemed like when I was playing there the wind always blew in from right field, or over towards left in a crosswind pattern. When the elements weren't against you it was a good park to play in because then it was a hitter's park. Back then Wrigley Field was looked at as just another ballpark. It didn't have that whole feeling of being a throwback, or a romantic ballpark. It was just another park and there were a lot of old parks that were in use in my time. The wind wasn't your friend and the sun was in your eyes.

My first year I played mostly center field, but after that I moved mostly to right field. I am better remembered for playing right, but I did play center at the beginning. Billy Williams started out in right field, but he was having problems over there, so they switched him to left and put me in right. It takes time for young players to get used to playing right field in Wrigley. You have the sun, the wind, and the brick walls on the side and in back of you. Down the line in right there is little space between the field and the brick wall.

Rookie year my roommate on the road was Tony Taylor. Tony was a second baseman from Cuba who made two All-Star teams during his career. He played in the majors from 1958 to 1976. Tony was a guy who helped me out more than anybody else. He was the one who showed me the ropes in the big leagues, places to eat, stuff like that. He got me a place to stay in Chicago with one of his Cuban friends, who lived next to him in an apartment building.

My first wife was of Hispanic heritage, and Tony was instrumental in getting her acclimated a little bit. He had some Spanish-speaking friends and they became friends with her. That helped her relax a bit in big Chicago after living in the small, quiet town of Pueblo, Colorado.

Tony had only been with the Cubs for one year before I came up, but he knew everything from having been around the league once. I went out with him when we were on the road. He knew where to go. Tony was a nice guy, really nice. Everything was new and fresh for me. I hadn't seen the other National League parks.

The era of baseball was quite different when I broke in as a rookie. The weather was not so great for opening day and there were only 12,000 people there. Now the Cubs sell out every game just about no matter what the weather is. Wrigley was just one of many old ballparks in the National League at the time. It's just that over time all of the others have gone away. Pittsburgh had Forbes Field. Cincinnati had Crosley Field. The Phillies were playing in Connie Mack Stadium. All of those parks had been around for a while, so the fact that Wrigley was old wasn't unique. The Giants had been playing in the Polo Grounds before they moved to San Francisco. The Dodgers were playing at Ebbets Field when they were in Brooklyn. But when they first moved to Los Angeles they spent a few years playing at the Coliseum, which was used for the 1932 Olympics. Chavez Ravine didn't open until 1962.

Forbes Field looked gigantic the first time I saw it. I remember Bill Virdon playing in center field and it was 420 feet to the wall. It seemed like he was playing me in downtown Pittsburgh. I remember hitting balls about as far as I could and he ran them down. In later years I used to see him at golf tournaments and I got on him about catching up to so many of my hits. I told him I would have batted ten points higher every year if he wasn't out there.

The biggest stars in the National League were Willie Mays and Hank Aaron. Willie Mays was a once-in-a-lifetime talent. The guy could do it all. But then Hank Aaron made it look so easy. He wasn't spectacular like Willie, but he could do all things, run, catch, throw, steal bases. But he did it in such an easy fashion that you'd hardly notice how great he was. Willie had a flair about him. He was running the bases with his cap falling off. Even at the plate Willie had a way of setting up pitchers. The guy would throw a pitch inside and Willie would fall back. Then the guy would throw that pitch again and pow! It's gone.

I was around Ernie Banks all of the time so I watched him hit a lot. The first time around against a pitcher, maybe even the first two times, he took the first pitch and maybe the second pitch. Then, the next time he was up, with runners on base, he would hit the first good pitch, resulting in extra bases most of the time. Ernie was setting up that starting pitcher for later when it really counted. A lot of guys are first-ball, fastball hitters. I noticed that Ernie always took that pitch, even if it was down the middle. I'd be watching from the dugout and think, "What are you waiting for?" That kind of thing. But he was being patient, letting the pitcher work a little bit. In those days, the starting pitcher was still going to be in there when your turn in the order came around the third or fourth time.

Probably the greatest single day of hitting I had in the major leagues occurred my rookie year. On August 13 of 1959 we beat the San Francisco Giants, 20–9. We just kept pouring it on that day, hitting everything. It was a wild game. It was high scoring on both sides at the beginning. After three innings, the Giants were ahead, 7–6, and then we scored four runs in the fourth. We finally put it away when we scored six runs in the bottom of the seventh. I was hotter than the rest of the team. That game I went five-for-six with five RBI and three runs scored. I had two home runs and three singles. When you have a day like that you wonder why every day can't be like that. It was a typical high-scoring Wrigley Field game.

Other than Wrigley being a hitter's park when the wind was blowing out, it wasn't one of my favorite parks. It wasn't what you would call an "attraction" back then. I would just as soon that they had built a new ballpark when I was playing.

After the Giants moved to San Francisco, they moved into Candlestick Park. I liked playing in Candlestick. It was new and the wind favored hitting to right field. A lot of people complained that it was cold and windy there all of the time, but the way the wind blew was to my advantage. I loved the Dodgers' news stadium when it opened. By far it was the most beautiful. I liked the park, but it wasn't a good hitter's park.

Then the New York Mets came into the league and they opened Shea Stadium. Shea Stadium's clubhouse had carpeting and all kinds of modern stuff, and that was great. Before Shea opened the Mets played in the Polo Grounds. That was an historic stadium, but it didn't feel that way to me because the Mets were a new team, an expansion team. The Polo Grounds belonged to the Giants and Willie Mays.

My salary my first year in the majors was $5,000-plus, but in the middle of the season they gave me a raise. However, for the next year, the Cubs calculated my salary from the base without the mid-season raise. The Cubs would throw you a little bit of extra money, but then they would say, "Well, we've already done this for you so you have a raise." Players were at a complete disadvantage back then. You're sitting there negotiating with a businessman, the general manager. You're a rookie. There were no agents at that time. The organization had all of these statistics at its fingertips. They had the ability to point out your shortcomings and they always found something.

The team would be doing anything to save money and they made the case that you were lucky you had a job. It became a situation of "Where do I sign?"

7

Winter Ball in Cuba

By major league standards, George Altman's baseball background lacked depth. Although he began playing the sport as a youngster, the intermission in his career at Tennessee State cost him a couple of seasons of higher level playing experience. So after his rookie year, the Cubs suggested that he focus on winter ball to gain extra playing time.

Decades earlier, in the 1860s, Cuba had become one of the first Latin American countries to embrace the sport of baseball, one of the United States' most famous exports. University students taking part in the game returned to the island country after concluding their education and introduced the sport, and American sailors in port playing the game helped popularize it.

Unlike most Latin American countries which were devoted to soccer, Cuba differed in its fervent enthusiasm for baseball. Although many of the best Cuban players were dark-skinned and were not welcome in the majors, just like their American-born black contemporaries, Cuban stars competed in the Negro Leagues, and African American players often took part in winter league play in the tropics.

Probably the greatest Cuban player of all was Martin Dihigo, who flourished as a hitter, a pitcher, and later a manager, in the American Negro Leagues and in other Latin American countries. He is a member of the National Baseball Hall of Fame in Cooperstown, New York, but also is a member of Halls of Fame in several Latino baseball-playing nations.

Not long after Jackie Robinson broke the color barrier in major league ball by joining the Brooklyn Dodgers, the best Cuban players began breaking into the majors. Among these early Cuban players to make it were Minnie Minoso, who was the first black player with the Chicago White Sox, and the first black player for either Chicago big-league club, Preston Gomez,

Mike Fornieles, Camilo Pascual, Pedro Ramos, and Altman's friend Tony Taylor.

Despite this long love affair with the sport, after Fidel Castro led the Communist revolution and took over as dictator of the country, he also slammed the door on the American professional leagues. Under Castro's rule, and subsequently his brother Raul's, Cubans have not been allowed to pursue making a living in professional ball. This policy has been in effect since 1961. Some of the last Cuban stars who came to the U.S. before the crackdown was under way included Tony Perez, Luis Tiant and Tony Oliva. In recent years numerous key members of the Cuban national amateur team have defected to the United States in order to play professional baseball. One of the most recent stars to emerge after leaving his country of birth, is Cincinnati Reds pitcher Aroldis Chapman, who made his first All-Star team in 2012.

When Altman went to Cuba to work on his game, it was one of the last times American players were allowed to do that. He also played for one of the great winter league teams of the time. According to a Sporting News story about the annual Caribbean Series, "The Cubans presented possibly the most formidable club ever to appear in the Caribbean Series."[4]

The Cubs asked me to go to Cuba in the fall of 1959 into the winter of 1960. The team and I both recognized that I had not had enough experience and they wanted me to play more and make up for the years when I didn't play. I ended the 1959 season on a high, hitting like four home runs in the last six games, so the Cubs saw potential in me.

Castro came down from the hills and invaded Havana on New Year's Eve of 1958 and he took over the government on New Year's Day. When I went to Cuba the Communist revolution wasn't a year old yet and Castro had not consolidated everything he wanted to do. The doors were still open for baseball, but not for long.

Cuba had always been known as a great place to play baseball. The caliber of play was super. They had some great players and there were a lot of players from the United States who went there. It was the No. 1 winter league for major league pitchers and players. The season lasted a few months and we played about 60 games. My team was the Cienfuegos Elephants. Unlike in the United States, we didn't play every day of the week.

The whole league was centered in Havana. All of the teams played there. Once in a while we played a game on the outskirts, out of town, but most of the competition took place in Havana. My wife Rachel came with me for a few games, but she didn't stay. She was pregnant and there was a problem with the food. She left early and went back to the States. I have always been interested in languages, and I picked up a little bit of Spanish at that time.

During that time period all of the Cuban guys who played on the big-league teams came home in the winter to play ball before their friends and family. They wanted to keep their names out there, and it was a way to make some extra money at a time when big leaguers didn't make very much. Playing baseball was a better off-season job than most people could get in the United States. Of course Minnie Minoso was there. So was Pascual and Ramos, Tony Gonzalez, Pancho Herrera and Roman Mejias.

The teams put the American players up in hotels. The single guys, anyway. At first I lived in an apartment with my wife, but when she left I moved into a hotel with the other guys. There were other American players there as well, other major leaguers like Jim "Mudcat" Grant and Jesse Gonder.

One thing that was nice about the entire experience was that I missed winter altogether. It was like living in Florida. There were palm trees and beaches and you know it seemed as if the people were happy-go-lucky. Before Castro showed up, or really put his hand into every-thing. When you walked down the street you heard music playing everywhere. It seemed as if there was a good time going on everywhere, all the time. Again, before Castro, Cuba was known for its night-life. A lot of Americans went there to spend time in the nightclubs and to gam-ble in the casinos. Havana was a wide-open resort town in the 1950s, but it shut down fast and most of the entertainment and gambling dis-appeared pretty quickly under Castro's regime.

Havana was also a late-night town. It didn't roll up the sidewalks at six P.M. or anything like that. When we played night games basically everything was still open after the game. After the games there were out-door pavilions where we could go dancing and have a good time. It was a fun place, a good times place, and I really enjoyed playing there. We only had three games a week so we also had a lot of free time to soak up the culture. It was a great way to spend a winter. Snow was non-existent.

Not only did I have fun there, but I also played very well. I hit a lot of home runs. The league home run record at the time was something like 16 and I was closing in on it when I tore up my ankle sliding into home with the catcher blocking the plate. I missed a lot of games in the second half of the season and that's how I missed the record, ending up with 14 homers. I batted .251 with 32 RBI and 41 runs scored, and that last statistic led the league. Lou Klein, who was a Cubs coach at the time, was the home-run record holder. The first thing he said to me was not hello, or how are you, but, "Aha, you didn't break my record." He was all smiles.

But I played in the Caribbean Series, with teams from all over Latin America competing. I did well in that Series despite having been out for nearly a month. I drove in the first two runs for us in the opening game and we swept all of our games. The Caribbean Series is very important in Latin America and it is a very colorful event. Fans come to the Series from different countries and they all sit together and play their music and sing their songs. It's really neat. Cienfuegos won the Series with a 6–0 record. It was the fifth straight year a Cuban team won the title.

Going to a new country was a treat for me. One thing you have to remember is that you are a guest in their country. A lot of Americans have been known to visit foreign countries and complain because it isn't just like home. That's foolish. If you wanted it to be just like home, you should have stayed home. It is critical for an American athlete to bring the right attitude with him when he goes to a foreign country to play. There are still a lot of Americans who play winter ball, even now, although you don't hear about it nearly as often. The stars don't go and those who make a lot of money don't go because they don't need paydays in the off-season. The major leaguers who play in the Latin winter leagues now are either Latin natives of those countries or guys who are farther down on the depth chart who want to improve their skills a little bit to improve their standing with their parent team.

These days, from what I read, you hear more about basketball players going all over the world, and not for the summer. There are a lot of great college basketball players who can't make it in the NBA, but who make a good living playing around the world. Since the Dream Team got started in the 1992 Olympics in Barcelona, every country seems to be improving in basketball. The very best players from those countries come to the United States and do make it in the NBA. That eats up jobs for Americans and instead they go overseas to play. When I played with the Cubs the difference was that I was overseas only in the winter to make myself a better player for the Cubs. The basketball players go overseas to have a career at all if they can't make it in the NBA.

Whether it was back then, or now (I assume it is the same), you can't be "The Ugly American" or the experience is not going to work out for you. You can't come with a bad attitude and be complaining all of the time. There are a lot of adjustments you have to make whatever country you go to. You have to adapt to their way of life. They don't have to adapt to you. The food is going to be different than what you are used to, for sure. And depending on where you go, most places, definitely there is going to be somewhat of a language barrier. It's just something you have to recognize and deal with. It's their country and you have to pay attention to the local customs and their way of doing things.

I played baseball in Panama, in Cuba, and in Japan. That same general rule applies if you want to thrive in another country. I saw guys who came and who did not exhibit the best behavior, especially in Japan, and the people there are very sensitive to how Americans act and treat them. I could see many ways in which it happened. Sometimes Americans would disparage the food, or just the menu, making fun of it.

In Cuba, before Castro took over, the beaches discriminated between haves and have-nots, between wealthy tourists and poor local people, and between blacks and whites. There were certain beaches that only high-class people were allowed to frequent. I was told that people of darker skin were not welcome there. There was a certain amount of discrimination in Cuba between black Cubans and the lighter-skinned Cubans. That was not something we could change. You had to realize that's the way it was in their society. You didn't have to like it, but you weren't going to change it during one winter, either. One of the things that made Castro popular in the beginning was that he was introducing policies that broke down barriers like that. He was speaking to the poor masses and he appealed to them with his promises of what he was going to do for them in daily life.

That year I played in Havana it wasn't clear yet just what Castro was going to be doing. He had been in command for less than a calendar year when I arrived. However, the exile community was already growing in Florida. Those were the people who fled from Cuba and settled in the United States because of Castro. It didn't take long for them to avow that he was a Communist, but at first Castro denied that he was one. Castro reigned in Cuba for decades and one of his trademarks was giving long political speeches on the radio and TV. He actually was already giving those when I was in the country. The players would be going to the ballpark in the afternoon, maybe four or five o'clock, and he was broadcasting over the radio and you could hear it over loudspeakers that were set up around downtown. Hours would pass and the game was over, and he was still talking, still going strong.

I was in Havana to play baseball, but it was a very political time. The Cuban exiles organized flights over the country and dropped leaflets saying that Castro was a Communist. There was also some fighting that broke out occasionally. I don't know who did it, Castro supporters, who attacked some of the people in Cuba with grenades and things like that. You'd hear about that and the next day in the newspaper you would see that people were injured and bleeding. The headline from the Castro-controlled paper would read, "United States Bombs Cuba." Of course that was definitely wrong. There were tensions that we saw. It was a time of change and we were witnesses to it, but the baseball was fairly normal.

We would go to the park, take our warm-ups and play the game. The fans would cheer as usual. Sometimes Castro would come to the games. He was known for being a big baseball fan and he had been a pitcher. There are stories that if the right scouts saw him he would have been a major leaguer, but I don't know anything about that. When Castro came there was a different atmosphere at the games, but that was because he was heavily surrounded by security people.

There were stories about how good a player Castro was, but I never saw him on the field. If he took the field in any winter league game, that was before I got there. Guys who had been there before told me that the season before I came there was even gunfire and stuff like that at games. At times there was fighting in the streets and they kept very close to the hotel. I didn't see any of that. Outside of the sporadic gunfire, leaflets being dropped was probably the most controversial thing I saw happen.

Cuba was a good place to play. I had a good time while I was there and the baseball was good. I would have been happy to come back and keep playing in future winters, politics aside. Even during that time there was a general mood of having fun with outdoor parties and music. But then Castro changed everything. Nobody was welcome to come from the United States anymore. Even the Cuban players couldn't come back. If they returned to their homes, then they wouldn't be allowed to return to the United States again to play ball.

This change affected some players that I knew like Tony Taylor, but they didn't talk about it much. It had to be hard for them to know they couldn't go home again if they wanted to be professional players. They chose their careers over familiar homes and family in many cases, but I'm sure it was a difficult choice for many of those guys. There was one player on my winter league team named Rogelio "Borego" Alvarez, a pretty big guy who was a right-handed hitter. He was with the Cincinnati Reds organization and he came over to the United States and played a very little bit for the Reds in 1960 and 1962. He had pretty good minor-league seasons and those brief appearances with Cincinnati, and then he went back to Cuba. The Washington Senators picked him up and he was supposed to be their starting first baseman — that's what the manager Mickey Vernon, said — but after Alvarez went back to Cuba they wouldn't let him out again. That prevented Borego from reporting to spring training and it cost him his big chance in Washington.

Somehow after that he got away from the island and played in the Pacific Coast League. It is said that the Mexican government helped him get out of Cuba, but Alvarez did not talk about what happened. He never made it to the majors again. Alvarez kept playing ball, though, all over the United States and in Mexico. He ended up spending about 18 seasons in the minors and played in more than 1,700 games.

Maybe Alvarez was a guy who could have had a great major league career if he could have had the normal chances without interruptions. Tony Perez and Luis Tiant had to make the choice not to go back to Cuba to continue playing in the U.S. when they were young men. They stayed in the United States in the off-season. They could never go back, although many, many years later I know Perez was allowed to visit his relatives. In Tiant's case, many years later, though while he was still pitching, his parents were allowed to visit him. They were on visitors' visas, but they never went back to Cuba after that. They stayed with Luis in Boston and they passed away in the United States. Those guys (Tiant and Perez) were smart if they wanted to play baseball, but they had to make family sacrifices. If they had gone back to Cuba at the start of their careers we would never have heard of them in the majors.

For me, just about everything went well in Cuba except spraining my ankle during the regular season and having the injury linger. I couldn't put any weight on it without pain, and that affected my swing. I also came home with the beginning of mononucleosis and a kidney infection, and both of those things took me right into spring training. So Cuba was a great all-around experience, but then I came out of there sick and it really slowed me up with the Cubs for the coming season.

8

Getting Used to the Majors

After putting together a solid rookie year as a surprise roster invitee out of spring training, George Altman had improvement on his mind for the 1960 season. He believed a year of experience would help him better cope with National League pitching, and although injuries held his participation down to 119 games that season he was a better all-around player when he was in the lineup.

In 1960 Altman batted .266 with 13 home runs and 51 RBI. In 1961, Altman slugged 27 home runs, with 96 RBI, a .303 batting average, and a league-leading 12 triples. He also made the National League All-Star team that season.

In 1962, his fourth season with the Cubs, Altman hit 22 home runs, drove in 74 runs, stole 19 bases, and batted a career high .318. He made his second straight All-Star team that summer.

Altman's old friend and advisor Buck O'Neil joined him with the Cubs, becoming the first African American coach in the majors in 1960. That year the Cubs finished with a terrible 60–94 record that marked the team's 14th straight losing season. A few months after the campaign ended, Cubs owner Philip K. Wrigley made a startling announcement that was unprecedented in major league baseball annals then and is still the only attempt at such an unusual experiment. Beginning with the 1961 season, Wrigley said, the Cubs would no longer be run by a manager, but by an eight-man committee of coaches that became known as the "college of coaches." Coaches took turns running the team as acting managers. This was one of the craziest setups baseball has ever seen, and it did not improve the Cubs' fortunes. Altman was one of the regulars during this period.

However, despite the strange doings on the club's masthead, during this early 1960s period immediately following his rookie year, Altman

George Altman (left) always appreciated the coaching and life lessons imparted by his Kansas City Monarchs manager, Buck O'Neil (second from left) and the man who steered him to the Cubs. Also pictured, "Bebop" Gordon (center), former Cubs star Billy Williams (second from right), and Ron Teasley (far right). The group gathered in Phoenix, Arizona, in 2006.

played some of his most memorable games. One game he remembers very well and one that he is most proud of was the day he handled Sandy Koufax with surprising ease. Koufax was in the prime of his Hall of Fame Los Angeles Dodgers career.

One day I was not scheduled to play against the Dodgers, who were throwing Sandy Koufax, but at the last minute I was put into the lineup. I ended up hitting two home runs against him.

The date of the game was August 4, 1961, and we were playing them at the Los Angeles Coliseum. I went three-for-four with three runs batted in and two runs scored, which is a great game against anyone, but an even bigger game against Koufax. I hit a solo home run in the fourth inning and a two-run homer in the sixth inning. We won 4–2 as "Big" Bob Anderson out-pitched Sandy on this occasion. Bob was one of the many young Cubs pitchers with great promise who somehow failed to live up to their potential in the long run. It was a pretty special thing getting two home runs off Sandy Koufax in one game.

Another good hitting game I had came against Vinegar Bend Mizell. Mizell was a pretty tough left-hander who played mostly for the St. Louis Cardinals, and I hit two home runs off him in one game, too.

When I played with the Cubs there weren't a lot of amenities. Meal money was cheap. Flying everywhere by jet plane was just starting and teams did not have their own planes. No way. Players don't know how easy they have it now. One way you knew you were in the big leagues as compared to the minors, or even the Monarchs, where we rode buses everywhere, was how your luggage was handled. With the Cubs when we were finishing up a series against one team and we were on the road and moving on to another city against another team, we would take our bags to the ballpark, and the next time you'd see them was in the next city's hotel lobby. You didn't have to carry them. In the minors and with the Monarchs you had to handle your own bags.

When you're starting out in the majors there are things you have to learn for yourself no matter how much teammates try to fill you in. Luckily I learned one lesson in spring training, not in a real game where it didn't cost my team. I was on second base and I considered myself to be a pretty fast runner. One of the next batters hit a hard shot to center field. I took off and I thought, "Hey, this is going to be easy." I just knew I would be safe by a mile. Next thing you know when I'm sliding into home plate, the guy is standing there holding the ball. Whoa! The catcher says, "Hey, rook, that's Willie Mays you're running against."

That's how I learned not to run against Willie Mays, or Roberto Clemente, for that matter. One day against the Pirates I singled to right center. Since the ball was not hit directly at Clemente I took a big turn around first base. I saw that Roberto had the ball, so I headed back to first. As I was about to step on the bag I felt the breeze from the ball as it passed my head. The first baseman was barely able to catch the ball since he was a little late getting back to the base. I thought, "Wow! What an arm!"

One reason I was so happy to hit those two home runs off Sandy Koufax was because he was actually the hardest pitcher for me to face. Juan Marichal was tough because he had six or seven different pitches that he could throw over the plate. A little bit later on Bob Gibson was one of the toughest for me. Warren Spahn was a super control guy. He had a very high leg kick and he had great control of all his pitches. He'd throw the curve over the outside corner and then he'd throw the fastball under your chin. The leg kick made it harder to pick up the ball coming in on you. I had a few hits off of him, a home run here or there, but you can't make a living hitting off Spahn.

It was always interesting for me to play against the Giants. Sam "Toothpick" Jones was one pitcher I hit pretty well. I got lucky off him a couple of times. But another reason I hit well off Jones and the Giants in general was that they had Willie Kirkland and Leon "Daddy Wags" Wagner on the team, my old Army buddies. They used to tease me all of the time and yell things at me. They got on me about different things. Wagner used to make fun of my skinny legs. He called me "Little Stalk." That meant I had legs like corn stalks. So I really wanted to do well against those guys. They motivated me.

I think it was my first year with the Cubs that the Giants came to Chicago and they were one game the Dodgers and Braves for first place with only five games to go in the regular season. Sam Jones was pitching and it was late in the game, and they were leading by a run. I came up to bat with two outs in the bottom of the ninth inning and I hit a two-run homer to beat them 5–4, and that pretty much knocked them out of the pennant race. Before the game we had planned that Willie and Leon would come to my house for dinner afterwards, but after I beat them with the home run, they didn't come. They never showed up. Later, Leon said, "The reason I didn't show up is that I probably would have cut your throat. You're messing with my money."

The funny thing was that I wasn't trying to hit a home run. It crossed my mind briefly before I stepped into the batter's box, "What if I hit a home run?" I kind of wanted to see those guys win the pennant instead of the Dodgers because they were my friends. But Sam Jones threw that fastball up near my eyes and I hit it. Again, that was unusual because I was a low-ball hitter. But that pitch was right up there, served to me on a platter. What are you gonna do? You come to play the game.

The biggest problem I had throughout my major league career was injuries. It was one thing after another and it started my rookie year. I was in the field and I dove for a ball, and as I did the ball hit my right index finger and broke it. It's never been quite as straight again. It's a little bit out of kilter. I tried to play through it and ignore it, but it's hard to bat with a broken finger. I missed 19 games that season, but that was also because I had a few hamstring problems. I thought I could have had a better season. I was looking for a little bit more. I broke the finger in mid-season and I was hot at the end of the year.

I was very impressed with our hitting coach, Rogers Hornsby. Hornsby was one of the greatest hitters of all time with a .358 lifetime batting average. He had retired decades earlier and he had managed some, although he always had trouble with the players. He could be a cranky, grumpy guy. When I ran across him he was nearing the end of his baseball days, and, in fact, his life. Hornsby coached with the Cubs from 1958 to 1960 and he died in 1963.

But he liked both me and my roommate, Tony Taylor. He said me and Tony were the only guys who listened. We were young guys and I guess the older guys on the team didn't pay that much attention to him. Hornsby was a fabulous hitter. He hit over .400. That's why I listened to him, a guy like that. Hornsby used to say, "Wait on them. Wait on them." Of course you've got Koufax out there pitching and he's throwing 90-to-95 mph, what are you talking about, waiting on him? You do have a tendency when a guy like that starts the windup to start moving. Koufax was the fastest guy around back then.

Koufax was just so hard to hit. It wasn't all his fastball. He had the best curve. He had movement on his pitches. He could throw a low pitch and the ball seemed to rise up. Most guys throw a high fastball that seems to rise, but it seemed like he threw a low pitch that rose from the speed. He had a big curve. If he was getting the curve over, you could mail in your at-bat. He was just reaching his prime when I came up. He hadn't quite mastered the curveball. He wasn't getting it over the way he wanted to yet, so he was relying on fastballs.

The next game after I hit the two home runs off him, Koufax probably got me out every time. That's the thing about baseball. One day you're oh-for-four and the next day you're four-for-four. Some of that is based on who the pitcher is on a given day. It is rather amazing that you are considered a big success if you hit .300 and you realize that's only getting three hits in ten tries.

You've got a round bat and a round ball and the pitcher is changing speeds. The curveball is another equalizer with the batter. Most guys can hit the fastball, but the curveball is something else. The biggest thing I found out later about the difficulty of hitting was that every hitter at times has a tendency to turn his head just a little bit. The first time you see the ball and identify the pitch you think, "I'm going to kill this." In your mind, it's "I'm going to kill the ball. I see it coming. I'm going to kill it." And then you just miss it. It's just a matter of by a quarter of an inch that you miss the ball. Sometimes it doesn't even matter if the batter knows what pitch is coming. In 1960, the Cubs had an injured catcher by the name of Cuno Barragan sitting up in the scoreboard calling out the pitches in a game Sandy Koufax was throwing against us.

We were sign stealing. Cuno sat up in the scoreboard and you could see him from the batter's box. If he raised up one foot that meant a fastball was coming. If he raised up both feet it was a curve. He was relaying the signs and it didn't do us any good at all. Koufax struck out 13 and pitched a shutout.

It didn't matter because what would happen is that as a batter you see that a curveball is supposed to come and I don't care if he's throwing it in the dirt, you're still swinging at it. A fastball? He's throwing it and in your eyes you're already starting to swing. That's why it's so hard to hit because even though you anticipate a pitch you still have to have the right timing. The first thing that goes through your head once you identify the pitch, you really want to crank it good. That's why a batting coach like Rogers Hornsby would be there saying, "Wait on it." You should identify the pitch and not try to kill it, just meet it. Just meet it means just take a nice, even swing. The jargon today is "Put a good swing on the ball."

The key thing is to identify the pitch and keep your head still. It is hard to do that if you overswing. Charlie Lau, the coach that was known as a hitting guru, stressed just keeping your head straight a little bit longer. He taught some unorthodox things like hitting off the front foot, but the main theme was to keep that head down and focus on the ball. If you can do that, when contact is made and the head is still, you hit the ball better and more consistently.

One thing that really helped me during my first years in the majors was my speed. It was no accident that I led the National League in triples in 1961 with 12. I was pretty fast once I got going. I had the fortune of never losing a race. I remember in spring training there were Sam Drake and Lou Johnson, guys who were really fast. Drake was a rookie and they said he was so fast that his feet didn't touch the ground. So once Johnson challenged him to a race and they asked me to referee. I told them I would run along with them to see who the winner was. I ended up running away from both of them. They were pretty angry with me. They thought I was trying to show them up.[5]

Between the 1960 and 1961 seasons I made a big leap in my batting ability. I became a .300 hitter for the first time. It all seemed to come together on an eight-game road trip that began at the end of May and continued into June. The Cubs and I got hot together. The team won seven out of the eight games and I batted .417 during that stretch. I drove in 13 runs during that streak, too, and my overall average coming out of that period was .356.

It was also the first time I had been healthy in a long time. My injury problems started with that sprained ankle in Cuba. Just when the ankle was getting healed, I re-injured it in the Caribbean Series and injured it a third time during the 1960 season. It took me a long time to get over the mononucleosis, too. I never did get completely healthy that year, and you can't do your best in baseball unless you are healthy. Being healthy makes all of the difference in the world.

9

Just Playing Big League Ball

During the early years of his major league career when George Altman was becoming comfortable on a big-league roster, the Chicago Cubs were one of the weaker teams in the National League.

The Cubs had a smattering of stars, in particular shortstop Ernie Banks, who twice won a Most Valuable Player award with a lousy club. Outfielder Billy Williams was just breaking in in 1960, and so was 20-year-old third baseman Ron Santo.

Richie Ashburn, who had been a star with the Philadelphia Phillies, joined the team that season, and so did Altman's minor league friends Lou Johnson and Sammy Drake. The Cubs were never consistent and in 1960 each member of the four-man starting rotation had a losing record. Glen Hobbie was the ace with a 16–20 record and a 3.97 earned run average. Nobody in the lineup hit .300.

Charlie Grimm, who had decades of loyal service with the Cubs as a player, coach and manager, held down the field boss job at the start of the season, but after they got off to a slow start upper management swapped him into the radio booth for announcer Lou Boudreau, who finished the season as skipper. The change didn't help much. The Cubs, who were 6–11 on May 4 when the in-house trade was completed, finished seventh, 35 games out of first place.

That was the year of the Pittsburgh Pirates. The Pirates won the seventh game of the World Series on a walk-off home run by Bill Mazeroski, one of the most dramatic blows in baseball history.

In 1961, P. K. Wrigley adopted his infamous rotating coaches plan, but although nine different voices were heard in charge that season, the Cubs finished at 64–90, just four more wins than in the previous season. They were only 29 games behind the pennant-winning Reds that year.

Only three coaches took turns at the helm in 1962, but the Cubs finished even worse, with a 59–103 mark and 42½ games out of first place. During that dismal campaign the Cubs drew just 609,802 fans to Wrigley Field and ranked tenth and last in the league in attendance.

Still, Altman showed he could do some special things when he was healthy enough to play, the iffiness of that being the chief aggravation of his major league career. Sometimes he performed yeoman service with the bat, but he also covered ground in the field, notably on a famous play in a May 15, 1960, game when a Cubs no-hitter was at stake.

Don Cardwell, who had just been traded to the Cubs, was pitching a no-hitter. The game was played at Wrigley Field and Cardwell, who was a right-hander, had come over from the Phillies two days earlier. We were playing the St. Louis Cardinals in Cardwell's first start for us.

We were ahead 4–0 in the ninth inning with the Cardinals at bat. When you are playing the field in those circumstances, you know it's a no-hitter and you want to work extra hard to preserve it. There's some pressure on you. You don't want to be the one that spoils it. Everyone in the field at least has the idea that they'll put forth a little extra effort.

As we came into the ninth inning, the only base runner had been the Cardinals' shortstop, Alex Grammas, who walked in the first inning. When Carl Sawatski came up in the ninth I was playing deep. I was very conscious of how close I was to the brick wall in right field. I was kind of fearful about having to go up against the wall if I had to make a catch, and sure enough Sawatski hits it hard and deep to me. I've got to make this catch. It was over my head and I was going back on it and when I got to the wall I jumped. I was very close to the wall. If I missed the ball it wouldn't have been a home run, but it would have hit right up close to the top of the wall for extra bases.

I jumped and caught it and the fans, who were all rooting for a no-hitter, gave me a big round of applause. So I saved the no-hitter, but that wasn't the end of it. The next batter, George Crowe, hit another fly ball to the outfield, to Richie Ashburn in center, for the second out. Up came Joe Cunningham. Joe wasn't really a power hitter, but he got a lot of base hits on line drives. He laced a shot to left field on a 3–2 pitch

76

and Walt Moryn came tearing in. At the last second he reached out and made a shoestring catch to end the game. So he saved the no-hitter, too. It was the first time in history a pitcher who had just been traded pitched a no-hitter in his first start for his new team.

Cardwell was an okay pitcher. He was never a really big winner, but he won 15 games for us in 1961. He had good stuff, but seemed to be a hard-luck pitcher.

In mid–May of 1960 I was just happy I was in the lineup after missing a lot of games at the start of the season. The ankle problem that started in Cuba also became a knee problem. I think I started having knee pain because I was favoring my leg because of the sprained ankle.

I thought I was in better shape than most of the guys in the major leagues. I used to work out harder than most other guys. As a matter of fact, Ernie Banks and some of the other players accused me of trying to show them up because of all the running and exercise that I did. But for me, I needed it. I knew what I was used to from playing basketball and that I had tight muscles that had a tendency to pull, and I wanted to stay as loose as possible. Ernie and Billy Williams were different. They were more relaxed. They had different types of muscles. I studied kinesiology about fast-twitch muscles and slow-twitch muscles. I was more like a track sprinter who had fast-twitch muscles, and that told me if I wasn't careful all of the time I would pull muscles. It could be very frustrating.

The worst part of getting injured was that in those days there were always players who had a tendency to accuse you of not wanting to play. They'd say, "You're jaking." That's ridiculous because your performance, your livelihood, how much you get paid, depends on your performance. You can't play, you can't get paid. Even some of my teammates would imply that I wasn't really hurt. I remember Ernie came up to me a couple of times and said, "Are you gonna play today? Are you well? Are you hurting?" It was evident that I shouldn't have been playing. I was hobbling.

Management seemed to have the outlook at the time that you weren't really hurt and should be playing all of the time. Those were the days before agents, too, and the team would put pressure on you to play when maybe you shouldn't, and you had nobody to speak up for you.

One of my first friends on the Cubs was Tony Taylor, but some other new players came along when I did or soon afterwards. Ron Santo and I were teammates for a while. Lou Johnson, whom I already knew in the minors, joined the team. Lou Brock came up and spent time with us before he got traded to St. Louis. Billy Williams and I were roommates on the road.

As a team the Cubs were integrated if you looked at the names on the roster. We were integrated in that we had white players and black players. But we weren't truly integrated. After the game most of the white players would go their way and black players went their way. We always roomed with other black players. What I'm saying is that I didn't get to know Ron Santo quite as well as I might have liked. We had interaction on the field and in the dugout, and once in a while we played cards in the clubhouse or on the plane. He was quite a bit younger than me, too, and single. But one thing you could tell right away was that he was a talent and that he was going to play.

In 1961 the team introduced the College of Coaches instead of having a manager. It was a weird arrangement and they changed bosses constantly. It wasn't as big a problem as it could have been for me because I was a regular in the starting lineup and regardless of which coach was in charge he played me in right field. I remember it was a bigger problem for Lou Brock, who was a rookie. One coach might like him and use him every day and another coach might take him out of the lineup. It was hard to know what to expect. One of the coaches, Charlie Metro, told Lou that if he made a mistake he was coming out of the game. He didn't need that type of pressure on him. I was playing every day, so they didn't bother me.

One great thrill I got as a teammate was watching Ernie Banks play every day. He was tremendous. I watched him set up those pitchers and I marveled at how he hit those line drives through the wind when it was blowing in strong at Wrigley. The wind would hold up a lot of players' fly balls, but because he had that good wrist action Ernie hit line drives and it didn't bother his shots as much.

Any good baseball man could see that Brock had raw talent, raw potential. I don't know why the Cubs weren't able to develop him. I think he had too many people giving him advice or handling him in different ways. I know that Charlie Metro's philosophy was that he had to keep the players angry and upset. He felt we played better that way. That wasn't the case with everyone, particularly with a young player like Brock. With me it didn't matter. I don't think it mattered to Ernie. As long as they put you in the lineup, you don't care too much about who's managing. They can only say so much, like when to bunt, call for the hit-and-run, or steal bases.

Billy was so good because he had that great swing. They always called him "Sweet Swinging Billy Williams" and it was true. It was very smooth and then all you saw was the ball jumping off the bat. Ernie was Mr. Cub, but I don't think Billy was really in his shadow. They were different personalities and Billy proved he was a great hitter, too. He ended up in the Hall of Fame.

One thing that the fans never really knew about Ernie, beyond his interviews with the press showing how sunny his disposition was, is that he talked all of the time. He talked to the opposing hitters when they reached first base. He talked to our infielders. He talked to us on the bench. Ernie talked all of the time. He was always talking, period.

Baseball was a bit rougher game when I broke in. The pitchers threw at you to let you know who was in charge — like Don Drysdale my first time up. Infielders seemed to be spoiling for a fight with base runners around second base. They might try to tag someone extra hard and the runner might come in spikes-up. The first time I saw something like that was when I was with the Kansas City Monarchs. There was a player with the Birmingham Black Barons named John Kennedy who had the reputation of being a very hard-nosed player, maybe a dirty player, because he was one of those guys who would slide into second base with his spikes high.

Kennedy, who also played with the Monarchs, was running around the bases and trying to reach home plate. He was called out at the plate and his manager came out to protest to the umpire. The manager had a reputation of being the type of guy who carried a knife, of being a real bad character. The manager was arguing with the umpire and the umpire turned his back on him, signaling like the discussion was over. Well, John Kennedy, who was standing behind them, kicked the umpire through the manager's legs. The umpire, who was wearing one of those old-style iron masks, spun around and hit the manager with it right in the face. The manager jumped the umpire and it took about six guys to get him off the ump. The police had to come out on the field to restore order. If that happened in a game in the majors now, everyone would have been thrown out of the sport for a year or more. At the time there was basically no punishment at all.

That was the biggest fight I ever saw on a diamond, but there were other fights and confrontations. The sport was just tougher. In the majors, a big confrontation took place at Wrigley Field when Billy Martin sucker-punched Cubs pitcher Jim Brewer and broke his jaw. Martin didn't like the fact that Brewer was pitching him way inside. His bat was somehow thrown near the mound. Brewer picked it up and was hit as he was giving it back to Martin — he was unaware Martin was in attack mode.

The whole College of Coaches thing was just peculiar. You didn't know what a manager might do on a given day, what he would say. One year they used nine guys to manage, but the next year when Buck O'Neil was in uniform they only used three. Buck never got to manage. His turn never came. They never got around to Buck and he was probably the best of the lot.

I was definitely looking forward to when Buck would take his turn as the manager. There was a play once when Charlie Metro was managing against the Phillies. There were runners on second and third and Bobby Wine, the Phillies' weak-hitting shortstop, was due up before the pitcher, Art Mahaffey. Usually you would walk the position player to get to the pitcher, but Wine was not a good hitter. Metro decided to walk Wine. Buck was sitting on the bench and you could hear him in that booming voice of his, "I don't know what you're walking that guy for. The pitcher's a better hitter than he is."

Bobby Wine's lifetime average was .215. I wonder if he ever got another intentional walk in his career. [Wine had a total of 53 intentional walks in his career.] Metro turned to Buck and said, "Buck, let me handle this. I'm coaching tonight. You'll get your turn. I'm handling now." I think Mahaffey hit a double or something and Buck said, "I told you so." Everyone talked about Buck getting his turn in charge, but it never happened. You can't tell me that was an accident. Baseball wasn't ready for a black manager, even one to lead for a few games.

Buck was the first African American coach in the big leagues, but it didn't really get that much attention at the time. Not the way it did when Jackie Robinson broke in or when Frank Robinson became the first black manager in the 1970s. People took note of it, but they didn't make a big deal out of it.

I was one guy who was glad to have Buck around the team and in the dugout. He was inspirational to us, just by his presence. He was also a cheerleader in a fun kind of way. He would cheer the pitcher on and yell things like, "C'mon, you're better than he is." An opponent would hit a ground ball and Buck would be on his feet, at the top of the dugout steps, saying, "Turn to the right." It was like he did play-by-play coaching, cheering you on. Everyone who has ever heard Buck, or who saw him in that Ken Burns documentary "Baseball," knows he had a huge, booming voice. So you could always hear him on the field. When our guys were up he'd keep up the chatter, saying, "Light 'em up! You can hit him. Light 'em up!" He was always encouraging.

When Buck was coaching with the Cubs he was the same as he had been with the Monarchs as manager. The players always liked Buck because he showed his enthusiasm all of the time and it was obvious he was always on your side. He always said things to encourage you: "You can do it," "Don't worry about it," "You can hit him." He's about the only coach I had who did that constantly.

The Cubs should have given Buck a turn managing, but I don't remember him ever complaining out loud when it didn't happen. When Buck was in the Ken Burns film he was in his eighties and he came off to audiences as a real mellow guy. He could be that way, but when he was a coach or manager when he was a little bit younger he could be more fiery. Or maybe emphatic. He would make his point strongly and loudly. That's one reason he was inspirational. He was always helping you, and he kept it up when you were out on the field. He never talked down to a player or criticized one in front of teammates because he spent all of his energy encouraging them. If he was worried about a hitter's concentration he wouldn't yell for him to pay attention. He would say, "What's he throwing you? What in the world is he throwing you?" That was his way to tell you to concentrate more. He was in the game all of the time, every pitch.

Buck never indicated that he was bitter because he was born black and couldn't play in the majors during his prime playing years. The name of his autobiography is *I Was Right on Time*. He chose that title because people would always ask him if he wished he had been born later, after baseball had been integrated. That was the answer he always gave to all of the people who asked if he was bitter on losing out and being unable to play in the majors even though he was a great player. "I was right on time" was always Buck's answer.

He said he was right on time because he played during the heyday of the Negro Leagues, when the teams were great, and in some places they outdrew some of the major league teams like the Washington Senators. He knew the great ballplayers were equal to, or better than, the great stars in the majors. But Buck always said that the rest of the players' lives in the Negro Leagues were pretty special, too. They went out and enjoyed the night life, went to the clubs to listen to Duke Ellington and all of the famous black entertainers. It was the heyday of mixing sports and entertainment. Those players played for the love of the game and they did love the game. They played it hard. They enjoyed it. So that's why Buck said he was right on time. He didn't really miss playing in the majors. Although he would have liked to have the opportunity, it was not something he anguished over.

I think it takes a man of a certain temperament to talk like that and think like that. That was characteristic of Buck and how he lived his life. He said he ate at some of the finest restaurants, stayed in some of the greatest hotels, and saw the greatest entertainment and got paid to play baseball. It's just that they were all black-owned hotels and restaurants and he had all black teammates.

When I look back at that period when the Cubs were run by the College of Coaches, I can't remember hearing anyone say it was a great idea. If you had the players, if you had the horses, it wouldn't have mattered much. But if they had the horses the Cubs probably wouldn't have tried it. Maybe if they had better people running it, it would have worked out better. Some of the coaches had no managing experience. Some of them were nice guys, but weren't cut out to be managers. I thought some of the things Charlie Metro did with his idea of keeping players angry were just silly. He did minor stuff to irritate the players. He took away clubhouse snacks and he didn't want us to use our shaving equipment in the locker room after a game. It was little petty stuff. Maybe if the Cubs had higher quality people as the coaches it would have worked out.

No one has ever argued that the experiment with the College of Coaches was successful. That may be why no one has ever tried it again either. When Leo Durocher was appointed as the new field boss, someone asked him if he was going to be head coach and he said, "I'm the manager." That was the last time anyone ever asked about rotating coaches.

10

Big Moments and Tough Moments

Even with stars in the lineup like Ernie Banks and Billy Williams and young players showing considerable potential like George Altman and Ron Santo, the Chicago Cubs never seemed to move closer to the top of the National League standings.

No matter how many coaches the Cubs used, the overall record did not improve. Lou Boudreau returned to the broadcast booth in 1961 and Charlie Grimm became a coach. Outside the Windy City, it was the Cincinnati Reds' year. The Reds won the National League pennant under manager Fred Hutchinson and represented the circuit in the World Series against the New York Yankees.

As bad as the Cubs were, winning just 60 games, the Philadelphia Phillies were much worse, winning only 47. Although there was hope that the team would move up, the Cubs were actually one game worse in 1962. However, Altman turned in his two finest seasons, hitting more than .300 in both 1961 and 1962.

These were the prime years in Altman's major league career, but given that he had come to the majors late after college, the Negro Leagues and the service, he was already pushing 30. By 1961, two things were apparent in Altman's Cubs career — he could swing a mean bat when he was healthy, and he had trouble staying healthy. "Big George ... shaking off injuries and ailments that retarded him the past two years, has come into his own not only as one of the kingpins of the Cubs, but as one of the swatsmiths of the game," one Chicago sportswriter reported in 1961.[6]

During the first half of that season, as the Reds began to show their dominance, the Cubs held them back, winning ten out of the first 16 encoun-

ters versus Cincinnati with Altman hitting .382 against the Reds. At one point when his average hovered in the .360 range, Altman briefly led the National League in batting.

The most frustrating aspect of my entire career was how often I got hurt. I had trouble staying healthy and it interfered with my play. Most of my injuries were smaller ones, not things that knocked you out for the season, but I had illnesses and sprains and things like that. I tried not to get discouraged and always tried to get back into the lineup as quickly as I could.

When I was healthy, though, I played well. My numbers were very good in 1961, with 27 home runs and a .303 average. I led the league in triples. I could always run pretty well, but the important thing was that I was mostly injury-free. That was a pretty healthy year.

My speed helped me get those triples, and my long stride enabled

During his seasons with the Cubs, George Altman became friendly with Ernie Banks (left), "Mr. Cub," and they occasionally visited one another's homes.

me to take the extra base. I was voted the fastest player on the team, though you know who was pretty fast? My good friend Tony Taylor. With triples, once you hit the ball you've got to come out of the batter's box running fast. Even if I hit a home run I didn't stand around to watch the ball. I left the box fast. When I hit all of those triples, some of them bounced up against the fences and bounced around in different ways, making it tough for the outfielder to pick up the ball. Sometimes the ball would hit the top of the wall and bounce around funny. Occasionally you would see hitters go into a home-run trot because they thought the ball was out and then have to pick up speed just to get a double because it didn't leave the park. I never did that. When I hit the ball, I was off and running. It so happened that year that a lot of hits turned into triples instead of doubles.

The 1961 season was the year I hit the two home runs in one game off of Sandy Koufax. Typically, I would have sat out the game because he was a dominant left-hander. So the night before the game I was out with some of my colleagues and their friends at their house. We went out to dinner and went back to the house. Anyway, curfew on the road was either 11 P.M. or midnight at the time, and I got back a little bit late. One of the coaches saw me coming in and said I was five or ten minutes late. With Koufax pitching I had no idea I would be playing, so I wasn't too worried about getting back to my room early. The odds were better that I would get fined for breaking curfew than of getting into the game against Koufax.

Then I ended up playing and playing well. I always say I don't know how I got the two home runs off of him, but I will always remember it. I think he was just throwing where I was swinging. It was errors on his part. The Los Angeles Coliseum was really a football stadium. The wall in left field looked so close. It looked like a volleyball net was just hanging there waiting for you to spike the ball over the fence. I'm sure pitchers just hated that because if you were a right-handed pull hitter it was in your favor. Even for a left-handed hitter, and with the Dodgers having a lot of fastball pitchers, you're going to swing late sometimes and you might hit the fence or hit it over. Even though I was a hitter, not a pitcher, I would have to admit that there were a lot of cheap home runs hit to left in the Coliseum. I hit one to left and one to right field. Hitters never say there is anything such as a cheap home run because you want to give

86

yourself credit for making contact. But you couldn't get full of yourself in Los Angeles because you know, hey, that was a bloop homer. That's what I called it. I don't remember if I got good wood on the one to left or not.

Koufax was pretty good back then, but he was not at his best yet. That came in the next few years. Still, I looked it up once and the only other player to hit two home runs off of him in one game was Felipe Alou. If the record is right that means that I am the only left-handed hitter to do it. So hitting two home runs off Koufax in one game is something that I'm going to remember the rest of my life.

One time when I was with the Cardinals I got three hits off Koufax in a game, but they were probably all singles and it was probably going 3-for-7 or something. It wasn't hitting two long balls. Most of the time Koufax had the advantage over the hitter. It was forget-it when you went up there to hit when he was getting that big curveball over. That's the one time that if you were going to come up with a hang-nail and not be able to play, you'd want it to be when it was Koufax's turn to pitch against you.

In 1959, when I was a rookie, I hit .245. My third year with the Cubs I batted .303, and that was very satisfying. I got off to a slow start and began hitting better and better. I was so hot that I was selected to play in the All-Star Game for the National League for the first time. It was quite a thrill. I ended up playing in the same outfield as Hank Aaron and Willie Mays. I went into the game for Roberto Clemente in the late innings.

It was a fantastic experience to be at the All-Star Game and to participate as a player. I was a fan as well as a player and I hadn't been a major leaguer for very long. To see all of those superstars in the dugout with you and to look out on the field and see Mickey Mantle and Roger Maris, it was quite a thrill to be playing with them all.

The winning manager of the pennant in each league the year before gets to manage in the All-Star Game the next season, so in 1961 the manager was Danny Murtaugh because the Pirates won the World Series in 1960. In those days the players in each league seemed to take the All-Star Game a little bit more seriously than they do now. Guys tended to stay with their original teams longer and they had pride in their leagues. Still, it wasn't as serious as a World Series game or a regular-season game where you are just trying to take care of business. If I remember correctly, in Murtaugh's clubhouse speech before the game he said, "All right guys, go out and get them ... because if I have to make decisions, you're in trouble!" He was joking, just saying something humorous, and trying to get everyone to relax.

During that time period the National League pretty much dominated the All-Star Game. There was more pride in representing your league at the time, but I think the National League did so well because it had a lot more black ballplayers. We were on a roll then. Look at some of the African American stars in the National League, including Aaron, Mays and Clemente. Plus Ernie Banks. I used to look at the old records of games played before Jackie Robinson broke the color barrier and I thought, "Oh, that was way back there B. C." Before color, that's what we used to say. The black players used to make comments like that. When old records were discussed, we believed that if some of the stars in the Negro Leagues had been allowed to play, those records may have been altered a bit.

For a couple of years when I was playing, they held two All-Star Games each year. In 1961 I played in both of them. The first one was played on July 11 at Candlestick Park in San Francisco. I pinch-hit for Giants pitcher Mike McCormick in the eighth inning and the pitcher for the American League was Mike Fornieles, a reliever for the Boston Red Sox. I had played with Fornieles in Cuba and I remembered that he was known for being a breaking ball pitcher. The first pitch to me was a curveball and I hit it. Bam! It was gone, over the right-field wall for a home run. I was fortunate I was up against a pitcher I was familiar with. I sped around the bases because I felt my socks beginning to slip and I did not want to be embarrassed on national TV.

To me a big part of hitting is studying. I tried to remember all of the pitchers. In Japan, where I didn't even know the opponents' names, I used to keep a diary of what the pitchers threw to get me out in a particular game and how they pitched me, the way the ball was moving, and all of that stuff. I didn't keep a book in writing when I was in the majors, but I thought about it all of the time. My little diary was in my head.

When I broke in, there were only eight teams in the league, and then ten. You saw those other teams over and over again and they didn't have 13 pitchers on a team. They left the starters in longer and there were only four of them going every fourth day. So you got to know all of the pitchers and what they threw. There were always charts, or scouts and someone else, usually the manager or a coach, would go over the other team's pitchers with us before the game and remind you how they were likely to pitch you.

Pitchers threw a lot more complete games when I played. Now they go by pitch counts when they pull a guy out. But if a pitcher was going the distance you saw him throw a lot more innings. It was a good benefit for the hitters because you learned exactly what his pitching pattern was and you knew most pitchers had a tendency to wear down a little bit after seven innings or so. That meant that maybe the third time he had to go through the lineup you had a better chance of getting a hit if he got tired.

I think when I was playing the pitchers were more cunning. My impression of pitchers today is that as a group a lot of them throw harder than pitchers I played against. I think the earlier pitchers relied more on control than pure speed. These guys today throw a lot of fastballs. If you know a guy is going to throw mostly fastballs, I don't care how hard they are throwing, if you're a major league hitter you should be able to hit them, or at least make good, solid contact. If you were playing against Elroy Face and his forkball, or Stu Miller and his change-up, those guys were as hard to hit as the fastball pitchers. They would beat you with finesse. Anyone who threw a knuckleball was hard to hit, but we didn't see many of them. Barney Schultz threw a knuckler, but he was on the Cubs, so I didn't have to face him. One of the things about the knuckleball, about why it was so hard to hit, is that you saw it so rarely and never got used to it. Another guy who was wicked hard to hit against was Ted Abernathy. He threw from a submarine motion. I saw a lot of those types of pitchers in Japan.

Most of the real fast fastball throwers like Bob Gibson and Don Drysdale and Jack Sanford with the Giants never hesitated to knock you down. Those guys throwing flames had intimidation as part of their games. They didn't worry about hitting you, but their real purpose was to upset you and break your concentration when you were at the plate.

One guy on the Cubs— and this was a little bit later — whom I didn't want to bat against was Kenny Holtzman. He threw two no-hitters.

When he was on, he was very good. He won more than 170 games, but I thought he would win more. Maybe part of it was control and that he got too much of the plate a lot of times. But then he was also with the Cubs and the Cubs weren't winning, so that may have held his win total down, even though Holtzman later pitched with championship clubs in Oakland.

I also played in the second All-Star Game in 1961. I didn't start that time either and I got up to the plate once. I went 0-for-1 in that game, which was played a few weeks later, at the end of July, at Fenway Park in Boston. I couldn't top that pinch-hit home run in San Francisco.

11

Cubs Life

The 1962 season was a good one for George Altman. He batted a career-high .318 and made his second National League All-Star team. He also had a career-high 19 stolen bases.

Yet the Cubs made no progress with their 59 wins. There was a small group of very talented, very popular Cubs, but no matter how many poems Ernie Banks spouted, how effectively Ron Santo covered the hot corner, or how much Billy Williams kept on impressing people as a hitter, they were stuck near the bottom of the National League standings.

One thing the Cubs had no trouble doing was staying out of the NL cellar. This was a historically bad season for the expansion New York Mets. The Cubs finished 19 games ahead of the Casey Stengel-led club that ended up 40–120 and set the modern record for the most losses in one year.

The best team in the league that year was the San Francisco Giants, who with Willie Mays, Willie McCovey and Juan Marichal, won the pennant and took the New York Yankees to seven games in the World Series before losing. Losing was something that the Cubs knew too much about, and not even having guys like Altman turn in career-best seasons gave the team enough weapons to contend.

Even in the early 1960s Cubs fans loved their team, but there just weren't as many Cubs fans as came along in future generations to turn their worship of the franchise into an almost cult-like following.

It was good to be a Chicago Cub when I played, and that was because of Chicago Cubs fans. The Cubs were not very good on the field, but they had a loyal following, really strong, keen fans. It's not like it is now where everywhere you go fans would recognize you if you were walking down the street. That would happen sometimes, but not all of the time.

One of the things the Cubs of my era had going for them was broadcaster Jack Brickhouse. Brickhouse had his own following, too, because he was such a good commentator. But there weren't three million fans a year coming out to the ballpark. During September, the last weeks of the season, when we were way back in the standings and the kids were back in school, most of the time attendance was very sparse. There was a lot of room at Wrigley Field then.

Some of the current fans think it has always been this way, where it is so tough to get a ticket and the fans come out in big numbers even if the team is losing. But it wasn't like that then. It wasn't hard to get a ticket. Now you have to buy them months in advance if you want to see a game in person.

During the 1962 season I had another of those small injuries that bother you for a long time and hold back your performance even if you can still play some of the time. I slid into second base and sprained my wrist. That was probably one reason my home run production went down from 27 to 22. I didn't miss too many games that year, though. I played in 147 games and had 603 plate appearances, the most of my career. In general I played very well and again that was because I was mostly healthy.

My wrist did hurt if I swung really, really hard. Most of the time, I was just meeting the ball. I didn't hit the ball as far. I had pain when I connected, but I was trying to make solid contact, not hit home runs. I wasn't hitting the ball as far as I did in 1961. One of the players on an opposing team said, "George, swing the bat so we can get you out."

The biggest frustration I had throughout my career was not being able to stay healthy. Even in 1961 I missed 24 games and had to be patient about getting into the starting lineup. I just kept my mouth shut and kept working and the coaches noticed. "He never once complained," Harry Craft, one of the rotating head coaches, said. "He kept right on hustling to the hilt. He was the first one on the field every day and the hardest worker. He was simply biding his time and waiting for his chance. He was determined that once he got into the lineup, he wouldn't get out."[7]

One of the fundamental things lacking in my formal baseball education was learning how to slide properly. I had never really been taught, so I was always sliding on my buttocks and I had a lot of raspberries.

Those things are painful, so I got in the habit of putting my right hand down. When you're sliding you're supposed to keep your hand above your head and just slide on your leg and pop up. They call it a pop-up slide. I could never do that. I had never learned how. So I just kind of slid on my side and put my hand down as a cushion. And one time I bent my wrist back. My wrist hurt, but it didn't prevent me from doing the same thing again and again when I slid. So the injury lingered. Yet I tried to steal and I stole more bases that year than any other ever. There were more opportunities and management told me to run more often. They were trying to use my speed more and take advantage of it. I had shown speed on the base paths going from first to third and in the outfield so the theory was I should be able to steal more bases, which I did.

I hit .318 that year. The ball was just falling right. You have to be lucky sometimes. I made the All-Star team for the second year in a row. There were two All-Star Games again that year. The first one was in Griffith Stadium in Washington, D.C., and the National League won, 3–1, on July 10, but I didn't play. The second one was at Wrigley Field on July 30, and the American League won, 9–4. I was added to the team because Felipe Alou got hurt.

It was great to have the All-Star Game at home. The fans were fantastic. They gave an extra-special welcome to the Cubs players. I only played as a pinch-hitter. I think I flied out. We got beat by my old buddy Leon Wagner, who went three-for-four and hit a home run. I ended up playing in three All-Star Games over two years. That was the last year that they played two All-Star Games in one season. In 1963 they went back to the old way and they've stuck with that schedule ever since.

It is definitely an honor any time you are selected to play in the All-Star Game. These days you hear about some guys who are trying to get out of playing in that game. I just can't see why those guys wouldn't want to go. It's a special thing to be chosen, whether it is by your peers or by the fans. It means you are being recognized for doing a good job. Who wouldn't want that?

One of the oddest things that happened during an All-Star Game in 1961 was Stu Miller being blown off the mound at Candlestick Park. To me, at the time it barely registered. Maybe I was used to the gusts of wind in San Francisco every time we played there, but it didn't seem like a big deal. Stu was not a big guy (5-foot-11, 165 pounds), but he wasn't that little, either. It's pretty amazing that more than 50 years later people still talk about that happening. It did not really stand out to me at the time. It just happened. When you played at Candlestick you got used to wind gusts blowing paper and dust and other stuff around, but they were gusts. It didn't blow hard all of the time.

The wind was another reason I idolize and respect Willie Mays so much. He played all of those home games at Candlestick and had to contend with the wind with all of those balls he hit high and deep to left field that were taken by gusts of wind and stayed in the park.

That 1962 season I probably had more confidence in my hitting than at any other time. Not being injured and batting over .300 changes your outlook. A big part of hitting is confidence. You get the momentum going and it's a lot easier. When you're in a slump you tend to try too hard and tend to think too much. You're always going, "What am I doing wrong?" You're thinking about how you're holding your hands. You're thinking about your feet. All kinds of stuff. All this extra information is running through your mind and you're not really concentrating on the ball as much as you should be. You're thinking about holding your shoulder in or whether or not you're over-striding. If you're hot, everything comes naturally, and if you're not you're thinking about what's wrong.

Although 1962 was my best season, I had my worst start. So did the team. The Cubs started 1–9 and if possible, I was worse than that. I went 0-for-10 in the first three games and after ten games I was 6-for-38. That slump was demoralizing, but it wasn't as bad as it seemed because I was hitting the ball fairly good. It was just a lot of hard luck, me hitting the ball right at somebody. There was a lot of that going on during that period. While I was a bit down because I wasn't getting on base, I was confident that things were going to get better. I was swinging well, considering. Even if you know you are making good contact, though, it still drives you nuts. You need the ball to fall in. When you have a few bad games and you take the collar, you always start getting advice from people. The coaches make suggestions. Advice is always readily available, and it is well meant, but a lot of times it is not all that good. Everyone else thinks they have the answer to what you're doing wrong, but most people don't. It can cloud up your mind, too. Sometimes what they say is helpful, but sometimes it just gives you more to think about. It takes away from your concentration.

One thing about me and hitting is that I always needed a lot of practice to stay sharp, a lot of work. I remember reading about Ted Williams taking hours and hours of hitting practice. I always wanted to be able to do that, but in those days the Cubs didn't have those kinds of facilities where we could just hit and hit. The first time in my career anywhere that I could hit as much as I wanted to was when I went to Japan. I think that was one of the problems with the Cubs—that we didn't practice more. When Leo Durocher became manager he thought it was a waste of time to take so much batting practice. But every player is different, and I felt I needed a lot of batting practice. That was just his philosophy.

The Cubs had some very good players, even great players, while I was with the team, but we didn't have enough of them and we always seemed to come up short in pitching. During that time period, until the National League expanded in 1962 with the New York Mets and Houston Colt .45s, who later became the Astros, there were only 16 teams. Every team had good ballplayers. It was a lot harder to make a major league roster then than it is now when there are 30 teams. Every team, even the weakest teams, had an All-Star who was a household name. We had Ernie Banks, who was one of the best players in the game, one of the best players ever. Billy Williams and Ron Santo also became Hall of Famers. So did Lou Brock, though for his work with the Cardinals after we traded him.

No matter what we did, or no matter what P. K. Wrigley did, the Cubs always seemed to end up near the bottom of the league. One theory was that playing all day games at home took a lot out of you during the hot summers. I tend to agree with that theory. By the end of the 1962 season I had been with the team as a regular outfielder for four seasons and I thought I had done pretty well. I had two .300 seasons under my belt and I made two All-Star teams. In 1962, I led the team in average at .318 and led the team with 19 stolen bases, a .393 on-base percentage and a .511 slugging percentage. Not bad, I thought. I wasn't going to be Ernie Banks, but I thought I had done a good job for the Cubs and I felt I was at home. And then, all of a sudden, I wasn't a Cub anymore.

I was part of a six-player trade between the Cubs and the Cardinals and I was off to St. Louis. The trade was made on October 17, only a couple of weeks after the end of the 1962 season, and the Cubs made it because they needed pitching more than they needed my bat. To say that I was shocked would definitely be an understatement. I didn't expect it at all. Players say the first time you are traded is the biggest surprise you get in your career, especially if you are playing well. Hardly anyone ever expects it. I had expected to remain a Chicago Cub, but I was now a St. Louis Cardinal.

The trade caught me off-guard, and I don't think I ever heard from Cubs management officially. I don't remember getting a phone call telling me that I was traded. I know nobody called me up and said "Thanks for your good work, you were an All-Star for us." Nothing like that happened. I actually think I heard about the trade on the radio.

I definitely didn't want to make the move from Chicago to St. Louis, but I respected the Cardinals organization, and the Cardinals team, so at least I felt I was going to a good team. It just was such a big surprise to be traded. No matter what kind of job you did for the team — and I believed I represented the Cubs well — there is always going to be at least a little part of you that thinks you were not wanted. Just like that, less than three weeks after the 1962 season, I belonged to another club.

12

Joining the Cardinals

Until shortly after the 1962 season ended, George Altman's only organized baseball experience was in the Chicago Cubs' organization. That included his minor-league days and four seasons in the National League. But he was now a St. Louis Cardinal, a member of the team that was the Cubs' fiercest rival.

The Cubs sent Altman, Don Cardwell, who had pitched a no-hitter for them, and Moe Thacker to St. Louis in exchange for pitchers Larry Jackson and Lindy McDaniel, plus catcher Jimmie Schaffer.

Thacker was also a catcher, a backup for his entire five-year major league career. The 65 games he played for Chicago in 1962 were the most he played in a single season. Thacker appeared in only three games for the Cardinals in 1963 and never played in the majors again after that season. His lifetime average was .177.

The key figure in the trade for the Cubs was Jackson. During a 14-year career, Jackson won 194 games and made five All-Star teams. He was a regular in the Cardinals' mound rotation for years, but his finest season came in 1964 with the Cubs when he won a league-leading 24 games. McDaniel enjoyed a 21-year career, winning 141 games and saving 172, one of the finest relief pitchers of his era. In 1963, when he joined the Cubs, McDaniel finished 13–7 with 22 saves and a league-leading 48 games finished. Schaffer, like Thacker, was a career second-string backstop. He played two years for the Cubs, getting into 57 and 54 games, respectively. His lifetime average was .223 in eight seasons.

Chicago newspapers caught up to Altman when the trade was made for his reaction, and he made it clear he had wanted to remain a Cub. "I hate to leave Chicago and the Cubs," he told Windy City sportswriters, "but you accept being traded as an occupational hazard. They were wonderful *to me, the management, Mr. Wrigley. I couldn't ask for better treatment. I'll miss Ernie (Banks) and Billy (Williams), though."*[8]

Becoming a member of the Cardinals could have been construed as a step up in the baseball world, however. Historically, St. Louis had been a stronger franchise, but hit a fallow period in the 1950s. The Cardinals were stocking up for a fresh run, and the 1960s would turn out to be a very good stretch for the club. Altman hooked up with a team that won 93 games in 1963 and was loaded with talent. It was Stan "The Man" Musial's last year in a Hall of Fame career, and the Cardinals' everyday lineup was as good as any in the game, although the team fell short of the Los Angeles Dodgers by six games in the season standings. Ken Boyer, Red Schoendienst, Curt Flood, Julian Javier, Tim McCarver, Bill White, Mike Shannon, and Dick Groat were some of the players who competed for the Cardinals that year. Among the pitchers were Bob Gibson, Curt Simmons, Ray Sadecki, and Ernie Broglio. Despite the formidable lineup, Altman became a starter in right field.

He did have his usual off-and-on moments at bat. Moe Thacker said the Cardinals shouldn't have fretted when Altman was in a slump, though, because he was bound to get hot. "You don't have to worry about George," Thacker said, "because he's been that kind of hitter, cold for a while, then hot. And when he's hot he's one of the better hitters in the league."[9]

When I was playing there was no free agency. No one had no-cut deals or no-trade deals. If they wanted to trade you, they could trade you. There was nothing you could do about it until the rules changed years later. The Cubs had a lot of good sticks with Ernie Banks, Billy Williams, Ron Santo, Lou Brock and me. They needed arms. That's what it was all about. The Cardinals needed one more outfielder.

The Cubs and Cardinals were rivals and we always drew big crowds when we played them. A lot of people who became Cubs fans in recent years don't even remember that before Harry Caray became the radio announcer for the team, he was already famous for doing that job in St. Louis with the Cardinals. Harry's first big-league announcing job was with the Cardinals in 1945. He also broadcast for the St. Louis Browns before they moved to Baltimore and became the Orioles, but by the time I got there Harry was announcing for the Cardinals again.

I think Harry was one reason the rivalry was so big. People in central and southern Illinois used to listen to Cardinals games instead of Cubs games, but they would come to Chicago for the Cubs when the Cardinals were scheduled. That just helped build it all up. The people in those cities might like the Cubs second-best. Most fans like winners best of all. Unless you win so much you get to be a target or represent a goal for achievement for everyone else where they can say "We have arrived," if they beat the best. The Yankees are a case in point.

Quite surprised when he was traded to the St. Louis Cardinals for the 1963 season, George Altman made some life-long friends, although he played for that team just one year.

The Cardinals were a better team than the Cubs were, but at the time I was still reluctant to go to St. Louis. Part of it was that I was pretty settled in Chicago with my family. I think my wife was pregnant at the time, too. Plus the fact that the surroundings were all familiar and I was coming off a couple of successful years with the Cubs. I just hated to be uprooted. It didn't feel like a good time all around to go to another team.

However, the Cardinals treated me really well from the moment I got there. They were expecting big things from that team and they expected big things from me, too, since I hit .318 the year before and made the All-Star team. They put me right into the middle of the lineup. I can't say it was a mistake or not, but at the time I joined the Cardinals I spent my free time at home studying to become a stock broker. That's what I thought I wanted to do when I retired. Most of the preparation was done at home, and with my wife and kids upstairs I retreated into the basement to do all of my studying. The light wasn't very good there and it affected my eyes. I had to get treatment for them on my way to Florida to join the Cardinals.

I left for Florida at night and panicked when I left the bright lights of the city and hit the dark, lonely highways. I had trouble seeing the road signs and the lane lines. I stopped in Nashville to have my eyes examined. The doctor said, "Son, you need glasses and should get them as soon as possible." My vision seemed to improve a bit in the bright Florida sunshine, but it was not back to 100 percent. So I wasn't seeing the ball as well at the plate as I should have been. Early in the season I tried playing with glasses, but they were uncomfortable and steamed up in the humid summer air. I did better without them.

I was one of those guys who felt he should be prepared for life after baseball. You have to remember I wasn't that young when I reached the majors, so by 1963 I was already 30. I had read a lot about becoming a stock broker and I thought I might be able to take advantage of my name in the sport to make a career after baseball. I was investment conscious, anyway. So I spent my off days studying, took the test to get a license that year and passed it. It was a national test. It was a pretty stringent test in those days. I don't know how tough it is to pass now. I hurt my eyes some and I was sure it was from the minimal light in the basement. My hitting did fall off that year. Although I played in 135 games, I only hit nine home runs and drove in 47 runs, and my average was down to .274. Those were drop-offs in every category for me from the 1962 season with the Cubs.

The Cardinals were the Cubs' arch-enemy on the field, but as soon as I switched teams I made good friends with several of the players. Bill White was the guy I was closest to. What a career he had. He was not only a very good and smart player, he later became president of the National League for five years. Bill was an eight-time All-Star who batted in more than 100 runs four times. He was a great fielder around the first base bag. I was friendly with Bob Gibson and Curt Flood, too.

I didn't have too much interaction with Stan Musial, but I had seen plenty of him in my first few years in the league and I really respected him. He had such a great career. The guy batted .331 lifetime and won seven batting titles. It's hard to top that. It wasn't that he wasn't friendly with the other players, but in the clubhouse he always seemed to be surrounded by the newspapermen. They always wanted to hear his opinion. Plus, they knew it was going to be his last year so they gave him a lot of attention. He deserved it. He was a very nice guy, very gracious. Looking back on it, what I probably should have done was tried to talk to him about hitting. I think I missed an opportunity there. Then he was gone after that season.

When we traveled, Bill White was my roommate. That's how we became such good friends. Bill was a very smart guy, with strong principles. He let you know how he felt. He helped me out a lot when I came to the Cardinals. He introduced me to some people that became friends. He gave me tips about pitchers and what he knew about them. He got me to relax. He was just a good companion.

My first professional baseball was with the Kansas City Monarchs, and we encountered prejudice. I didn't have too many problems in the Cubs organization or with the team, but St. Louis was the southernmost team in baseball at that time, and the Chase Hotel in St. Louis was notorious for not housing black guests or letting black players eat in the dining room. For a long time the African American players weren't allowed to stay there. So that was one thing we all knew about St. Louis. Being with the Cardinals and having a home in St. Louis meant we didn't have road trips to St. Louis which required us to stay at the Chase, which was changing its policies. I did not suffer any overt prejudice in St. Louis, but sometimes remarks were made that gave you a feeling and made you turn your head. When the Cubs first stayed at the Chase when I with the team, they still had the rule of no African Americans eating in the dining room. They were slow to get with the program.

At first my wife, who remember was of Hispanic heritage, stayed in Chicago. I was aware enough of the segregation in St. Louis that when Rachel came to visit me I had trepidation about what we might run into. It was better for her to stay in Chicago while she was pregnant, and that was part of the reason she didn't come to St. Louis initially.

On the field the Cardinals were a very good ball club in 1963. We came in second and we were right there with the Dodgers until late in September. They came to town and beat us three games in a row. They were all pretty close games, 3–1, 4–0, and 6–5. That just about killed us. At home, too. We lost three more in a row after that to the Cincinnati Reds and the Cubs before we won one. By the end of that streak there were only four games left in September and it was too late. The Dodgers sweeping us put a damper on our aspirations. Up until then we thought we could win the pennant. We put ourselves into the race by winning 19 out of 20 games right before the Dodgers showed up. I had a nine-game hitting streak during that run.

In the first game of the series, Los Angeles started Johnny Podres, a left-hander, and he handcuffed us with just three hits in eight innings. I didn't play because our manager, Johnny Keane, wanted to use a right-handed hitter, so he put in Charlie James. The next game Sandy Koufax shut us out on four hits for his 24th win of the season, and I didn't play that game either as Charlie James played right field again. James went 0-for-6 in those games. In the third game the Dodgers started Pete Richert, another southpaw. James started again and went 1-for-5. I got in late in the game as a pinch-hitter and made an out. I can look back on those games against the Dodgers and say I wish I would have been able to play the entire series.

My average did drop that year, and a lot of it was the physical eye strain I went through studying for my stock broker's license. But some of it was probably mental, too. There was a lot of tension that year with my wife at first living in Chicago and me wanting to make good and make a good first impression with the Cardinals. There were times my vision was weak enough that when I looked out everything was fuzzy.

I still got off to a good start with the Cardinals. I was hitting .366 after a few weeks and someone from the front office came down and said that they wanted me to pull the ball more. In Chicago I hit to all fields and that's how I was hitting in St. Louis. But in those days, if you were a big, strong guy, and I was 6-foot-4 and 200 pounds, they thought you should be a home run hitter. They always wanted you to pull the ball and be that guy hitting a lot of home runs. I guess I was egotistical enough at the time to say, "Well, if that's what you want me to do, I can do it." I didn't do it. They said that Mr. Rickey is the one who thought up this idea. That's Branch Rickey Sr. He was back with the team as a consultant that year, in his 80s. Mr. Rickey was an idol of mine for what he did to help Jackie Robinson integrate the major leagues. He was a big celebrity and he said he was one of my admirers. He passed the word through general manager Bing Devine and it came down to me. I thought

I should give it a shot. I started pulling the ball, but instead of hitting the long ball most of the time all I did was hit a sharp grounder or something. The next thing I did was hit line drives. I'm trying to hit the ball in the air and I dropped my hands on the bat before taking my swing, which resulted in a hitch. From .366, in the space of like a month my average dropped to about .230. It didn't work out at all.

We finally gave up on the idea of me being a pull hitter. I went back to my old stance and my old style of being more of a contact hitter and trying to hit to all fields. The thinking at the time seemed to stress speed and hitting home runs if you were an African American player. That whole thing kind of put a damper on my year. It was really discouraging watching my average drop like that. The team had a very good year that season and I had to wonder how we would have done if I had had even my usual average year.

I liked Johnny Keane as a manager. I thought he was a good guy, a good manager. He was low-key. He wasn't a rah-rah guy. The Cardinals were owned by Augie Busch, owner of Budweiser beer, so at that time when you played for them they gave you a lot of free beer. It was hot and humid in St. Louis in the summer and you would sweat off several pounds a game. Also, when you got back from a road trip there was a case of beer waiting for you. It was one of the perks of playing for the Cardinals. The beer was free and I drank my share of it with all of the heat, and one day Johnny said to me, "Is this your normal playing weight?" I had gained some weight, so I had to ease off the beer a little bit. I hadn't been aware of it. Johnny brought it to my attention. Ordinarily I wasn't a big drinker, but being hot all of the time and having the free beer right there, I drank more than I normally would. I was just taking advantage of it.

Not only was Stan Musial in his last year, another Hall of Famer, Red Schoendienst, who was mostly a coach by then and would become the manager, was also around. There were definitely some veterans in that clubhouse. I wish I had talked to Red more about hitting, too, and when they asked me to pull the ball, too. I was on my own. I could have used some extra batting practice.

We had Bill White on first base, and he was my best friend on the team. Julian Javier was on second, and I had played Class A ball against him when he was in the Pirates organization. He was a nice guy. Dick

Groat had come over from the Pirates after their 1960 championship and hit .319 that year. Groat won the National League Most Valuable Player award and the batting title in 1960. You know he was 32 when he led the league with 43 doubles in 1964.

Ken Boyer was playing third base and he was terrific. He was our clean-up hitter. He was a very similar player to Ron Santo with the Cubs. They were the two best third basemen in the National League at that time. They were very, very similar in how they played, too. They were good fielders and good RBI guys. They won Gold Gloves, too. Boyer was a quiet leader on the team.

Tim McCarver, who became even better known as a TV announcer over all of these years, was a good, solid young catcher. He had been in the league for four years or so by then and he knew what he was doing. Musial was Musial. He was retiring, but he still commanded so much respect. When he retired he held the National League record for hits with 3,630.

I was with the Cardinals in the days before Bob Gibson really became famous, but you could tell he was going to be great. You knew if he was pitching it was always going to be a good game, a close game, even if he lost it. Gibson had tremendous stuff and didn't give up many runs even though he couldn't win every game. He was just coming into his own when I was there. He was also one of the best hitting pitchers out there. He was an all-around good athlete. He played college basketball like me, with Creighton in Omaha, Nebraska, and then he played with the Harlem Globetrotters.

Gibson could be tough on the mound. He had a nasty demeanor. He pitched inside a lot. He was like Don Drysdale, exactly like that, in that he didn't care if he hit the batter or not. He wanted to make the case that he owned home plate. Those two were famous for that approach, but there were a lot of pitchers around like that in those days, that had that style. When Gibson was pitching, if a batter came up to hit and he fooled around outside the batter's box, you know, taking a minute to dig in and adjust and all of that, you knew that Gibson was going to throw the first pitch at him, that the pitch was going to be right under his chin. Gibson's attitude was, "Get in the box and let's get it on." You delay and you would just tee him off. Whoosh! And if the ball happened to hit that batter, well, too bad. As I said, Gibson was just coming into his own. But we had Curt Simmons, too. He was a good pitcher and he was 15–9 that year.

I was not happy with the year I had after coming over to the Cardinals. I didn't feel that I had shown what I could do. When you get to a new place, for me anyway, it takes time to adjust, almost like coming to a team as a rookie. Everything is new and tense and I was trying to be a world beater. I wanted to have another chance to prove myself in St. Louis. I felt I would be more much relaxed and could do a good job for them the next year. I was sure I would have a pretty good year.

The sad thing is that the Cardinals kind of gave up on me and I only spent one season there. I didn't get that second chance in St. Louis. In 1964, the Cardinals pulled it all together, won the pennant, and won the World Series over the New York Yankees. By then I was in New York, too, but I was playing for the Mets.

13

On to the Mets

George Altman spent only one season with the St. Louis Cardinals before being sent to the New York Mets. The Mets debuted in 1962 when the National League expanded from eight to ten teams. The Mets were supposed to replace the New York Giants and Brooklyn Dodgers, who had vacated New York's boroughs to move to California in 1958.

To win favor with the fans, the Mets brought in former New York Yankees general manager George Weiss, who had helped build the Yankees' dynasty of the late 1940s and 1950s, and manager Casey Stengel, who won ten pennants in 12 years with the Yankees, a performance that was good enough to gain him entrance in to the Hall of Fame.

The popular management hires were one thing, but on the field the Mets were woeful, legendarily so, going just 40–120 in their inaugural season. They were permanent cellar dwellers in the National League, even worse than the Cubs at their worst, during the early 1960s.

In November of 1963, after Altman's debut season with the Cardinals, he was shipped to the Mets along with pitcher Bill Wakefield for starting pitcher Roger Craig, the old Dodgers hand. The Mets weren't much better than they had been in the beginning by their third season, and in 1964 they finished 59–103. Wakefield went 3–5 for the Mets that year, his only major league season. Craig, who had been with the Dodgers for World Series championships in Brooklyn and Los Angeles, had been lost to the Mets in the expansion draft. After seasons where he finished 10–24 and 5–22 with the horrible Mets, being sent to St. Louis must have felt like being rescued.

At one point, hurling for the Mets, Craig lost 18 games in a row, one short of the major league record, but when he was swapped for Altman, Craig said, "My two years with the Mets were a blessing." He said he used that word because it taught him to cope with adversity.[10]

Famed sportswriter Red Smith took one look at the trade and proclaimed that the .274 Altman hit in St. Louis may have been a disappointment to the Cardinals, but to the Mets, with their team average of .219, "a .274 hitter looked 12 feet tall."[11]

Life with the Mets in their early years was theater of the absurd. Some called it a circus with Stengel as the ringleader. Stengel was a funny but shrewd man and he frequently offered humorous observations about his players and team. His commentary could sting, too. Famed New York City columnist Jimmy Breslin wrote a book about the team titled, "Can't Anybody Here Play This Game?" The consensus answer was no. Altman went from what turned out to be the best team in baseball in 1964 to the worst team.

The Mets of 1962 set the standard by which all major league teams have been measured for worsts since then. The Mets' 120 losses in a season is a modern record, and the team was outscored, 948 to 617. The Mets also committed 210 errors that year. George Altman's 1964 Mets weren't much better, although they lost only 103 games. The Mets were outscored that year, 776 to 569, and committed 167 errors, still more than one per contest.

One of the legends of early Mets teams was Marv Throneberry, the first baseman who was not known for his skills with the glove. Yet in 1976 a bald Throneberry showed up in beer commercials. With a self-deprecating sense of humor, he said he was worried about Miller because if he did for beer what he did for baseball, the company's sales might go down.

Weiss, the Mets' president, spoke up for Altman after acquiring him. "Actually, Altman didn't have that bad a year with the Cardinals," he said. "It's just that he realized so much was expected that when he got off to a slow start he began pressing."[12] Altman said the biggest problem he had was tampering with his swing and hitting approach.

Another expert was polled about Altman's likely value as former Cardinals teammate Stan Musial chimed in "Altman is a good hitter. He got to pressing with us and just had a player's off year. He'll hit .300 for the Mets this season."[13]

In contrast to the types of multi-million-dollar salaries current players receive, Altman was paid $30,000 by the Mets that season. That's why he wanted to become a stock broker as an off-season job.

By the time Altman arrived in New York, much of the humor revolving

around the Mets had worn thin and it was more difficult to deflect attention
from the continued losing. The only one left in uniform who could still
make everyone laugh was manager Casey Stengel.

Casey Stengel was a managing legend, but he definitely could be a
very funny guy, very comical. He also could be pretty hard to understand
because when someone asked him a simple question like, "Casey, what
did you think about the game?" he would still be talking 15 minutes later
if no one stopped him. It might not even be about the game by that
point, either. He just talked circles around people. "Stengelese" they
called it, like the guy had his own personal language.

In a way he did have his own language. He knew what he was talking
about, and if you listened closely enough you knew that what he was
saying made sense. Once, we were playing in the Polo Grounds and Frank
Thomas was at the plate for the Mets. This was an earlier Frank Thomas
who was a power hitter, not the Frank Thomas that played with the
White Sox later.

The old Frank Thomas was a dead-pull hitter and he was our third
baseman at the time. He came to the plate with runners on first and
second with no outs. Baseball dictates that you try to hit the ball to
the right side to move the runners over. A consummate pro would
address getting the runners over. I think we were one run behind in the
game. But Frank, being the pull hitter he was, tried to go for a home
run. He hit the ball directly at the third baseman and he hit into a double
play. We lost the chance to score there and we lost the game. That was
that. After the game a sportswriter went up to Casey and asked him
about the play. He said, "You were so close. You could have won that
ball game. You were right there." And Casey said, "Yeah, we could have
won it except we had a player who wanted to be a sailor." Nobody could
understand what he was talking about. What it was all about was this:
down the left-field line there was a sign hanging there that said, "Hit
this sign, and win a boat!" That was Casey's way of saying that Frank
was too busy trying to hit the homer to left instead of hitting the ball to
the right side.

I never had too much trouble figuring out what Casey was trying
to tell me when he spoke to me. On one of the last days of spring training
I dove for a sinking ball and I dislocated my shoulder. Another frustrat-

ing injury for me. I injured my right shoulder and had to sit out. After a week I was feeling a little bit better, but I still couldn't hit anything. My hand didn't grasp the bat properly and I couldn't hit above my waist with any authority.

We were opening the season and Casey came to me and said, "I'm putting you in the lineup." I said, "I don't know. I don't think I can go." He said, "Well, I'll tell you what. You're better than anybody else we've got to put in down there." I told him I couldn't swing at any pitch that was above the waist with any kind of bat speed. But he talked me into it and I went in to play, anyway. The first few weeks of the season were not good for me. I couldn't get any speed on the bat. My injury was like that of the third baseman for the Cardinals recently who went to the Reds, Scott Rolen, the All-Star. He sat out for two months with his injury. I sat out for a week. I never felt 100 percent all year.

I played 124 games for the Mets that season, but I only batted .230. I think the shoulder problem is why I couldn't hit. During the first few years of the Mets, a lot of great players at the end of their careers passed through. They were reliving old glories in New York. Some of them came and went before I was even there, just playing one last season. If all of the Mets players had been there in their primes it would have been a good team. Instead the early Mets were kind of the laughingstock of baseball for a couple of years. Richie Ashburn passed through there. So did Duke Snider, Gil Hodges, and Jimmy Piersall to name a few.

There were some young Mets players just breaking in who didn't have experience and earned it the hard way, like second baseman Ron Hunt. Hunt was a throwback type of player. He sacrificed his body for the team quite often. He used to get hit by more pitches than anyone. Ed Kranepool was another young guy who probably got rushed to the majors. Joe Christopher was there and he had a good year, batting .300. Christopher was the first player in the majors from the Virgin Islands. He was a little different guy. He was always talking and he had a different philosophy than most of us on any number of subjects, and especially hitting.

It didn't matter how guys thought, if they could hit. I used to say that when you were at the plate the thing you had to do was stay back, keeping your weight back until the last second and not turning your head too soon when you swung. If you could do that, you would be fine.

A few guys lifted their front leg when they got ready to swing. Mel Ott, the old New York Giants player in the Hall of Fame, did that. But that was more extreme than what anybody in the majors was doing at the time. Sadaharu Oh, the all-time home-run leader in Japan, was famous for that style. This was a technique that enabled a hitter to keep his weight back a split-second longer. At one time it seemed as if half of the hitters in Japan adopted this style in homage to Oh.

One thing that was pretty neat in 1964 was the opening of Shea Stadium. When the Mets were created they played at the Polo Grounds, the Giants' old stadium, for a couple of years while New York built them a new stadium. It opened in April of 1964 and that contributed to the popularity of the Mets. What no one could figure out back then was why the Mets attracted so many fans. The team was playing bad baseball, but the team was popular. That year the Mets had more than 1.7 million fans in attendance, and that was second in the National League. There was quite a bit of activity and fanfare that year, mostly because of the stadium. The construction costs were $28.5 million to build Shea, which was an enormous amount of money at the time. I read that was equal to $214 million in 2012 dollars. The ballpark was named after William A. Shea, who was a big-time New York

One season with the New York Mets was enough with a losing club for Altman, although he did enjoy playing for colorful manager Casey Stengel.

lawyer. He was the one who lobbied hard to get the National League to come back to New York. Another plus for fans was the 1964 World's Fair. It opened next to Shea Stadium and it was a big, big draw.

Right from the beginning I thought that Shea Stadium was going to be a good hitter's park. The thing that convinced me was an event near the start of the season. The scoreboard was built deep behind the outfield in right field and it was tall. We were playing the Cincinnati Reds and Vada Pinson hit a ball that hit the top of the scoreboard. I said, "Aw, man, this is going to be good." But you know the whole rest of the year I didn't see anybody else come close. Pinson was a very good player, but he didn't usually have that much power. He had good power to get 15 homers a year or so, but not for a blast like that. Pinson was a star, but he played in the shadow of Frank Robinson.

The Mets were three years old when I played there and they had the image of losers. At the same time, the fans loved the team and supported it. You don't see that kind of commitment in too many places when the team doesn't win games. I guess the theory was right that New York needed a National League team to replace the Giants and Dodgers in people's hearts and that there were enough fans to go around for the Yankees and a new team.

Losing is no fun, though, and I got off to a bad start because of my shoulder, so playing wasn't any fun either. Casey kept me in the lineup for about a month at the beginning of the season and then I sat out for about three weeks because it became apparent the shoulder just wasn't getting any better. Then when I came back my legs weren't in shape and right away I pulled a groin muscle. So then I had that problem. A groin injury inhibits your swing. It really restricts you when you have a groin injury. You can't pop those hips with a swing. I kept having injury problems. Later, somebody wrote a story about me where the headline was something like, "George Altman Should Have Been A Star," and it discussed all of the injuries I had. I just kept missing out on the chances for stardom when I was counted on to perform at my peak.

The 1964 season was a tough year for me. I had the injuries and then when I sat out I got out of shape. I was in New York with a new team and I couldn't relax. Another problem that sprang up that year was marital issues. My wife was a small-town girl and unaccustomed to the

111

big city, whether it was Chicago or New York. When the team was on the road she didn't have anything to do and she was bored a lot.

I was trying to hit off a bad shoulder and a bad leg and it wasn't going well. When the team returned from road trips I didn't feel up to going out on the town on dates with her, or really doing too much socializing of any kind. Things must have been hard on her too. We had two small kids at the time. It was a terrible year.

As for me making friends on the Mets, I knew some of the guys from crossing paths with them in the minors or winter ball. Jesse Gonder was on the team and I knew him from winter ball. Al Jackson was pitching and I knew him from the Western League. A lot of players came and went very quickly on the Mets during the team's early years. The team recycled them through and the older guys retired. Playing for a team that lost so many games was very hard. It was not unlike being with the Cubs when it came to winning and losing, just more extreme. You knew that over the course of a 162-game season the Mets just couldn't compete. We definitely didn't have depth and we didn't have enough talent.

I have a competitive nature and I had been on winners all of the way up to the majors, from a youngster through high school, in the Army, even in winter ball. Then I got to the majors and we were losing all of the time with the Cubs. I got sent to St. Louis and that was a one-year reprieve. Then it was over to the Mets, who lost all of the time. At this point, in the majors, you really want to be a winner. The whole world is watching you. To get beat night in and night out grates on you.

Casey Stengel was an attraction to the fans, though usually people don't buy tickets to watch a manager manage. He was funny enough that some people just wanted to see what he might do during a game. I'll tell you what he did sometimes. He fell asleep on the bench during games sometimes. He was getting up there in years. In the sense of game sharpness Casey was probably over the hill when he handled the Mets.

One game we lost to Houston lasted about 22 innings and when we got on the plane we were all just dead. It was very quiet on that ride home because most of the guys were sleeping. In the next day's paper there was a story that included a comment from Casey: "How can they sleep after losing games like that?" We were tired, that's why we slept. It wasn't as if we didn't care that we were losing.

The year with the Mets was probably the least amount of fun I had in baseball, considering the difficulties with my wife, me not hitting and the team losing. The best time I had all year was socializing with some relatives that lived in New York. I got to visit them and that was probably the highlight of the season. I had to look very hard to find a silver lining that year. I did enjoy my kids when I got to spend a little time with them.

On June 21 of that season, Jim Bunning, who later went into the Hall of Fame and then became a United States senator, pitched a perfect game against us. The Phillies won the game, 6–0. I didn't start, but I went into the game in the ninth inning as a pinch-hitter. I hit for Amado Samuel, our second baseman. I hit a sharp line drive down the right-field line and it was almost a home run. It missed by inches. The next pitch Bunning threw to me was about a foot outside and low and the umpire rung me up. He called it a strike, but I knew it was a ball. I may have broken up the no-hitter, but instead I just became one of the ten players Bunning struck out that day.

I once heard Bunning talking about that game, or maybe I read it, but he said, "That was the only scare I got during that game."

After I got traded to the Mets and settled into life in last place — something you never get used to — the Cardinals went on and won the 1964 World Series. I just missed out on that chance there. That's every player's dream and goal, and being with St. Louis in 1963 when we finished second was my best chance. A year later they won the championship.

In the middle of the season the New York newspapers were writing stories about how I wasn't hitting, and one writer said my batting was a symptom of the problem about how the Mets figured to be much improved, but weren't. Then the writer mentioned my injuries. When he asked how a good hitter can find himself, I said, "You can go a whole year. Sometimes you can go two, three years and then something happens and you find your way out."[14] I didn't want to go a year or more with hitting problems, that's for sure.

The season with the Mets had been miserable for a lot of reasons. The injuries always frustrated me and I felt I hadn't shown what I was capable of in New York. I wanted to come back and show what I could do. I was only 31, so I didn't feel as if I was ready to retire by any means.

I felt I could still play and that my main problem was just getting healthy and staying healthy. If I was healthy I just knew I could shine. I wanted to stay with the Mets and redeem myself. But that's not the way it worked out.

Of all things, the next development in my major league career — something that definitely surprised me — was being traded back to the Cubs for the 1965 season.

14

Back to the Cubs

It would have taken consultation with Jeanne Dixon or some other well-known seer of the time for George Altman to have any insight into his immediate future after his 1964 season playing for the New York Mets. The season had not gone well, and not for the first time Altman had been slowed by injuries.

However, he felt he would be at full strength for an encore with the Mets in 1965 and would regain his swing and do a good job for the club. But he never got the chance because that winter Altman was traded again, for the third straight season. Much to his surprise, though, Altman's new team for 1965 was going to be an old team — he was on his way back to the Chicago Cubs.

The Cubs made a straight-up deal of Billy Cowan for Altman on January 15, 1965. Cowan, another outfielder, broke into the majors with Chicago in 1963 and spent two seasons with the Cubs. He eventually played eight seasons in the big leagues with a lifetime average of .230.

Apparently the Cubs missed Altman and felt he could regain his hitting skills with a fresh start in his old home. Although the Cubs could not finish higher than eighth in the National League during the 1964 season, with a record of 76–86 they were far superior to the Mets. To Altman it was a case of rejoining old friends, but also possibly a team on the rise.

The Cubs still officially had in place their College of Coaches, but the experiment was in its dying days. Within a year after Altman's return to Chicago, the plan was abandoned completely with the hiring of Leo Durocher as manager in 1966. In his famous welcome-to-Chicago press conference not only did Durocher pour ice water on the idea that there would be any more rotating coaches, but he announced that the Cubs were not an eighth-place team. To his lifetime chagrin, the Cubs followed that statement up by finishing tenth.

Durocher was a my-way-or-the-highway type of manager who was a three-time All-Star as a player with the Brooklyn Dodgers and St. Louis Cardinals, whose playing career began in the 1920s and continued into the 1940s, and who was a member of four World Series championship teams. As a manager he was a fiery leader of both the Brooklyn Dodgers and New York Giants and was respected for his handling of the talents of a young Willie Mays. Although Durocher was noted for his set-in-cement ways, he was elected to the Baseball Hall of Fame for his managerial achievements.

I was pretty surprised to be traded back to the Cubs, but I kind of liked the idea since I still owned a home in Chicago. The Mets traded me to Chicago for another outfielder named Billy Cowan. He was more than five years younger than me and the Mets thought he had potential. The Cubs wanted my experience and weren't sure that Cowan was going to be a starter.

After my experiences of the two previous years with the Cardinals and the Mets, I was happy to be going back to Chicago. That's where I had most of my success. The Cubs didn't really announce it, but the College of Coaches was dead and Bob Kennedy was really the manager. He was a great guy and a fair manager. I started off playing well and I was hitting over .300.

But wouldn't you know it, I got hurt again. I was back in Chicago and I wanted to do really well, but I only got into 90 games that season because of injuries. And after my fast start I couldn't keep it up because I was hurt. I batted .235 that season. There was one game where we were playing against the Mets and it was a close game. I was put in as a pinch-hitter and I could barely walk because of a pulled thigh muscle. We were in the tenth inning and I hit a two-run homer off of Dennis Ribant to give the Cubs an 8–6 victory. Casey Stengel practically went crazy in the Mets dugout.

"He's a cripple," Stengel said after the game. "I was looking for him to hit a grounder. He never would have been able to run it out. I had the infield back on the outfield grass. Since that fella was a cripple I figured he'd be an out." I couldn't disagree with Stengel. I was a hazard if I had to run.[15]

Not being able to run kept me on the bench for almost half of the season. Another bad year. I had so many injuries over those few years, most of them to my legs and groin muscles, that one sportswriter said that my team was Blue Cross. I was excited to come back to the Cubs. I hit well in Wrigley Field. Although I was in my thirties by then, I was still pretty fast when healthy.

We were told that if we saw that the third baseman was playing deep we should try to get an infield hit on a bunt. We were supposed to look for that, especially in a close game. We studied the pitcher to see what his motion was like and depending on the situation if it was a close game, we would try to bunt our way on. One game the circumstances were right and I laid down a bunt. I wanted to get on base and help win the game. The bunt was okay, just fair, and I burst out of the batter's box and was running full speed to first base. Bam! I thought somebody shot me. I thought there was a sniper in the stands. I tore my groin, although I think they called it my thigh muscle in the newspaper. I tore it right off the bone. I was in agony on the ground. They had to take me off the field on a stretcher and take me right to the hospital. That injury was a killer. I missed most of six weeks and I never was at full strength the whole season after I came back.

I never experienced pain like that. It really was just like if you got shot the way I went down. I'd had some minor, low groin troubles before, a slight pull, a little bit of pain. You limp along back and forth. You can walk. You only feel the ache when you're walking or running. But this one, man, whew. It was also very demoralizing because I'd had about three years in a row with injuries. Back in those days nobody lifted weights. The philosophy was that baseball players didn't do that because they would get muscle-bound and it would interfere with their swing. But if I had the chance to do it over again I would have put myself in the best shape of my life to avoid those injuries. I wouldn't care what anybody said about overdoing it, or showing up the other guys. I would say, "That's too bad," and go ahead.

I did work out a lot and tried to stay in condition, but I guess it wasn't enough. Maybe some of it had to do with nutrition. In those days we were all hamburger eaters. Maybe if I had better nutrition I wouldn't have got hurt as much. There was no talk about nutrition or vitamins. I keep coming back to the word frustrating. The injuries were similar, but not identical, but some were really severe. It wasn't as if I got just a little pinch and it went away in a day or two. The worst part was the recovery, sitting around, not being able to do anything. I should have had surgery. Even after I rehabbed that injury, scar tissue built up there and it inhibited me.

The treatment was rest and ultrasound. That's all they did. I probably should have repaired that thing because for years every once in a while I could feel it. I might not have been doing the proper stretching when I was playing either. We didn't know too much about stretching back then, either.

Coming back to Chicago helped patch things up with my wife and we stayed together. The kids were very young at the time, but we were together all of the time again. The groin pull made it seem like a lost season. I only had 196 at-bats in 90 games. That reflects a lot of pinch-hitting and coming out of games early because I couldn't run. I didn't hit well when I didn't get enough at-bats, so that was another way the season was out of kilter.

I had to be a regular. I was an adjustment hitter. I needed at-bats to figure out the way teams were pitching to me. But when you pinch-hit you've got one chance to get that one good pitch to hit. Other than that, you're fishing. I wanted to have a special season coming back to Chicago, but I didn't. I wanted to give the fans at Wrigley the George Altman they remembered when I was hitting .300, but it didn't happen.

Bob Kennedy was out the next season and the Cubs brought in Leo Durocher as manager for the 1966 season. Bob Kennedy was a nice guy and Leo Durocher was the one who said, "Nice guys finish last." So he made sure he was not going to be mistaken for a nice guy. Durocher comes in and he starts yelling right away: "If you don't do well I'm going to back the truck up and ship all of you guys out!" That's when he boasted that we were not an eighth-place team. He was trying to say that we had too much talent to finish that low and he was going to lead us much higher in the standings. And then we finished tenth. We were worse with Leo than without him.

Leo had the biggest ego in the clubhouse and he wanted the team to revolve around him. He wanted to be the No. 1 Cub. He was even picking on Ernie Banks, Mr. Cub, at the time. Every chance he got he would bring up some young player from the minors or get someone in a trade and say that he was going to be the new first baseman. He tried to bench Ernie, but Ernie was always better than whoever they brought in and he won the job back. If Ernie made a mistake in the field, missing a grounder, Leo would be criticizing him on the bench. He would say Ernie couldn't move. He couldn't do this and he couldn't do that. "He ought to go home." And we're sitting there in the dugout listening to this stuff and Ernie is our friend and Ernie is the best-liked Cub in history.

When the Cubs announced that Leo Durocher was going to be the new manager, I was looking forward to playing for him because of his reputation as a guy who won. He was a baseball man and I figured that he would be able to recognize talent. I thought he would be able to see talent in me if I was healthy and that I was going to have a good year in Chicago.

At the very beginning Durocher treated me okay. I went to spring training in 1966 determined to win a regular job in the outfield, and when we played our first exhibitions in California he started me in left field. That was probably the high point of our relationship. I went to spring training competing for a spot against Wes Covington and Harvey Kuenn, but I was seen as damaged goods because of my injury pattern. I also showed up with a first baseman's glove in the hopes I could maybe do some work at that position. At one point Leo said I was one of the two hardest working guys in camp.

Leo Durocher could be nasty. He wasn't a players' manager. He didn't want to be your friend. He wanted to be the show. Even Ernie Banks, easy-going Ernie Banks, his star, he couldn't get along with him. If you were going well on the field, then Durocher was your man. But if you were having any trouble, he was very impatient. I started off pretty well in spring training. I was doing the .300-hitting thing. We started the season with a three-game series against San Francisco and I hit my first home run of the year. After the first few games I started to think, "This is going to be my year."

We lost the series two games to one and we stayed in California to play the Los Angeles Dodgers. Well, just like that I was out of the lineup, that quick. Durocher played Billy Williams in my place. Sometimes he used Adolfo Phillips. He kept sticking other guys in there. I was thinking I had had an OK series. That was another thing about Durocher. He didn't feel that he had to explain himself to you. He just made the moves and sometimes he didn't even tell you what he was going to do. He didn't talk to us. He might have said to the press something like, "We need some young blood in there," or something similar, but he didn't talk to me directly. This became the pattern of the year. I would play a series or not play at all.

The next series I would play, but then as soon as the series ended I was right back on the bench. Durocher was experimenting with a lot of younger guys, and I was upset because I felt I could still play and that was one stretch of time I was healthy. Then the age thing started coming up. I was 32 that season. So 1966 was not my season at all. I ended up playing in just 88 games for the Cubs and batting only .222.

Psychologically I was upset all of the time because I only got the chance to pinch-hit and play occasionally. That wasn't my speed at the time. I probably could have done a lot better had I been agreeable to that type of thing, but I definitely wasn't agreeable. I was a star in batting practice even when I wasn't playing regularly and wasn't hitting in games.

Durocher had the young guys in and out of the lineup, too. They got a chance to play more, but they didn't look good in batting practice. When I watched them hit, I thought, "How is he playing these guys over me?" I also thought Durocher soured on me a little bit because of my wife. She was Hispanic with fair skin. I sometimes thought Durocher believed I was married to a white woman and held that against me. In those days you weren't supposed to have mixed marriages. I think Durocher thought that way. It may or may not have been true, but that was my perception. I was looking for reasons and it had to be something. I couldn't point to any one reason why I wasn't playing, what he had against me.

One of the years I was back in Chicago we played four games against Atlanta. I didn't play in two of the games, but in another game I hit a pinch-hit home run and then in the last game of the series I hit two home runs. Then we went to St. Louis and I barely got off the bench. We faced Bob Gibson and he beat us. Nobody hit him. In that game I hit a line shot to left-center that was run down by Bobby Tolan. The next game I was on the bench. I said, "What's this?" I just felt Durocher had something against me. Playing for Leo Durocher was not a lot of fun for me. [The fact that three of the games in the sequence were against left-handed pitchers may have influenced Durocher's actions.]

I always had an off-season job when I played ball because our salaries were so low back then. It so happened that over the winter between the 1966 and 1967 season I worked for the Congress Hotel in Chicago, booking banquets, conventions and teas. One of the sportswriters caught up to me and wrote an article, and I said, "Maybe I should invite Leo in for tea. We could sit here and have tea and crumpets and talk about next year."[16] Given how things went the next year it probably wouldn't have done any good.

I really wanted to play, but when the 1967 season started it was a lot like 1966. I was still a pinch-hitter and I was still sitting on the bench. After spring training, but still in the spring of the season, the Cubs came to me and asked me to go the minors because they wanted to make room for a younger guy. I was kind of doubting myself at the time and I still wanted to play. I figured if I went to AAA I could get myself back together. So I said I would like to go, and I went to Tacoma in the Pacific Coast League. So it was back to the minors, and I did all right there. I lit 'em up for a while and I ended up almost challenging the home run leader. After two months in AAA, the Cubs called me back up. I thought, "OK, I'm ready to play now." I rejoined the Cubs and I sat there for two weeks and only got a chance to pinch-hit a couple of times. Next thing you know, they option me back to Tacoma.

Leo Durocher could be crazy even when he was making lineup changes. He'd decide on a pinch-hitter, me or Lee Thomas, and send us to up the plate, but he'd be back in the dugout complaining about his own move and questioning why he made it. To be a good pinch-hitter you need to have absolute confidence, and you'd get back to the dugout after swinging and hear what Leo said. He'd be pacing in the dugout after he sent Lee Thomas up and saying, "Darn! Why'd I send him up to the plate? He ain't worth two dead flies." He'd say that on the bench with everyone listening. "Watch him. Watch him. He's gonna pop it up." If he popped it up, Leo would go, "Damn! I told you so." You're sitting there listening to that so you know when you went up to the plate he was doing the same thing. That would just make you more anxious. You'd go up to the plate and you'd be thinking, "I've got to get a hit." You're nervous. You probably end up swinging at a bad pitch or something. It was not a relaxed atmosphere. Pinch-hitting is already a tough enough job to do anyway, but in that circumstance it's even tougher.

So I didn't spend a lot of time in Chicago in 1967. I got into only 15 games for the Cubs and had just 18 at-bats. I batted .111. It was my ninth year in the majors, but the last few had been a wash-out. My career had gotten away from me and it was obvious Leo Durocher was not a George Altman fan. I still believed I had a lot of baseball left in me as long as I could stay healthy. I was only 34 in 1967.

The highest I got paid for one season in the majors was $27,000, although the newspapers reported one year that I made $30,000. It's amazing to read about what players get paid now. Albert Pujols signed, what, a ten-year contract for $254 million or something before the 2012 season? More power to the players if the owners are crazy enough to give them that money. It just seems obscene. I kind of wonder if any player is worth that much money. Of course, I would have liked to make more. If I was playing now, after the couple of All-Star years that I had, I would be making millions of dollars.

I came along too early for the big money. It took players like Curt Flood with the Cardinals going to court to challenge the reserve clause, other players who came after him, and Players' Association head Marvin Miller, all combined, to create change.

At that point, in 1967, I was healthy. I didn't have any hamstring or groin pulls and I believed if I was in shape and healthy I could hit the way I had before. Looking ahead to the 1968 season, I had a meeting with Cubs general manager John Holland. He said to me, "We want to make some room on the roster. We want to take you off the roster, but we want you to go to spring training and you'll have a chance to make the team." I wanted to stay with the Cubs and I wanted to stay in Chicago, but that didn't sound like a great deal for me. It didn't really sound as if they were going to give me much of a chance at all to make the team. I definitely wondered what chance I'd have if Leo Durocher was still the manager, so I asked if Leo was going to be the manager and Holland said he was going to be. I said, "Well, you can count me out."

That was the end of my association with the Cubs, and what I didn't realize immediately was that my brief time in the lineup in 1967 represented the end of my tenure as a major league player after nine years on big-league rosters. But it was not the end of my baseball career. I was right. I could still hit if someone was willing to give me the opportunity.

It turned out that being to sent to Tacoma by the Cubs to play in

14. Back to the Cubs

1967 was a blessing in disguise for me. While I was disappointed that I was back in the minors, I did play well and that got me noticed. You can never tell what turns life will take, but being in the Pacific Coast League was the critical fork in the road that led to the next chapter of my baseball life.

15

Learning to Play Ball in a Different Language

Baseball dates to 1872 in Japan and the first team was formed in 1878. Before World War II major league players competed in exhibition games on tours of the island nation. Babe Ruth told a story about a gentleman who came to his hotel room door seeking an autograph. Although the man did not speak English, he proffered the ball. Ruth signed, but the man produced another ball and then another from the folds of his floppy robe. Ruth kept signing, the man kept pulling baseballs out of pockets and pouches, and Ruth burst into laughter.

Professional baseball is one of the most popular of sports in Japan. There are two leagues under the umbrella organization of Nippon Professional Baseball, the Central and the Pacific Leagues. Each league has six teams. A full season in Japan is 144 games, compared to the 162 played in major league baseball.

The first Japanese player to compete in the majors was pitcher Masanori Murakami, who played for the San Francisco Giants in 1964 and 1965. For many years the caliber of play in Japan was assessed as that of the American high minors, AAA in nature. Over time, as play improved, some of the best Japanese players were signed to pro contracts and made a splash in the majors. Pitcher Hideo Nomo was the first Japanese big leaguer in three decades when he joined the Los Angeles Dodgers in 1995 after success at home. Nomo pitched two no-hitters.

After establishing themselves in Japan, more than 40 players have become major leaguers, with mixed success. Hideki Matsui helped the New York Yankees win a championship in 2009. The greatest crossover star from Japan by far has been Ichiro Suzuki, who spent a decade with the Seattle

Mariners before being traded to the Yankees during the 2012 season. Suzuki was the American League Rookie of the Year, won a Most Valuable Player Award and two batting titles, and set a record with 262 hits in a season in 2004.

Japan's greatest baseball star overall was Sadaharu Oh, who hit 868 home runs from 1959–1980, more than American record-holder Barry Bonds. Oh won nine MVP awards and then embarked on a long career as a manager.

Americans in small numbers have gone to Japan for decades to sample the baseball life. Rules limit the number of foreigners allowed to play on the 12 Japanese teams, and those who opt for the chance to play in Asia often have difficulty adjusting to the language barrier, local customs, and food. Those who adapt can thrive. Those who feel out of place do not usually stay very long. Also, because Americans take up valuable space on the roster as foreigners, they must produce or they are likely to be kicked out and shipped home.

Among the most prominent American ballplayers who spent some time competing in Japan are: Mike Greenwell, Clete Boyer, Alvin Davis, Mike Andrews, Don Blasingame, Jim Gentile, Cecil Fielder, Davey Johnson, Bill Gullickson, Bill Madlock, Jim Lefebvre, Wes Parker, Joe Pepitone, Don Zimmer, Reggie Smith, Don Newcombe and Larry Doby. Newcombe, Doby, and George Altman are the only three players who played in the Negro Leagues, the majors, and Japan.

While Altman was playing in Tacoma after his demotion from the Cubs, he made the acquaintance of a scout named Cappy Harada, who asked if Altman would like to play in Japan. Altman gave it some thought and decided he would like to try it. It sounded like a better opportunity than going to spring training as a non-roster invitee with Chicago after what he had been through with the organization under Leo Durocher in recent years.

The goal for Altman was to demonstrate that he could still play at a high enough level to make a living playing baseball in Japan. After his meeting with John Holland Altman made the commitment to go to Japan, and starting in 1968, see what it was like to play for the Tokyo Orions.

At the end of the 1967 season I was healthy and I felt I could continue to play baseball. I wanted to continue playing baseball. Tacoma was good for me in the sense it was almost like a rehab assignment, although technically that's not what it was.

I hit around .280 with 16 home runs and I drove in a lot of runs. It wasn't the same as playing in a big-league city. Even though it was AAA in the Pacific Coast League, not all of the parks had good lighting, so it was harder to see when you were hitting. There were a lot of young kids pitching and they were still learning how to pitch, so they could be wild, and I was back to traveling by bus. The pitching and bus travel was just not what I was used to after all of that time in the major leagues. But I wasn't ready to quit the game, either.

The Chicago Cubs were my team, and just like that year when I was with the Mets, I wanted a chance to redeem myself with the club. I never felt like I got the opportunity to do that with the injuries and being sent to Tacoma. I had some chances, but I never felt I had the real opportunity to show what I could do over a period of time. I was confident I could show better than that. And I had good years with the Cubs.

Japan sounded intriguing and I gave it a lot of thought. Former major league players who played in Japan included Gene Stephens and Chico Fernandez, whom I met when I was in Tacoma. They told me it was an opportunity, and that there were good ballplayers over there. They thought it would be a good place for me to play. They enjoyed it over there after I told them I wasn't going to go back to the Cubs. After that Cappy Harada took over.

Cappy was associated with the San Francisco Giants and frequently attended Giants games. I had a lot of good games against the Giants, so he was aware of my abilities. He said Giants owner Horace Stoneham was glad to see me go to Japan if only to stop doing damage to his team.

My first contract paid me $22,000, but it was better than that because it also included living expenses like housing, and it had tax advantages. The apartment they had for me was not fancy by American standards, but it was really good by Japanese standards. Most Japanese, especially in Tokyo, which was so crowded, lived in a very small space. I had two bedrooms and a kitchen. Before I agreed, the Orions sent me a ticket to meet with a club official in San Francisco. We met at the airport. Harada was the middle man. He was selling Tokyo on me and he was selling me on Japan, although by that time I didn't need to be sold. I wanted to play. I was told that generally the parks were smaller than they were in the United States and I should do very well there. And if I had a good year I'd have a chance to increase my salary. That did happen.

I didn't worry too much about being the only American — they said they would sign another one — and not speaking Japanese. Fortunately, the players were a great bunch of guys and they took to me right away. They asked me all the time about the majors. They had read my credentials and saw the All-Star Games so I had no problem fitting in with them. They accepted me and expected big things from me. Some of the players knew elementary English, so we could communicate.

I took a course in Japanese before leaving the United States, so I knew a few words of the language. The team promised to sign another foreign player and that did happen. Yankees farmhand Arturo Lopez was signed. They actually thought they were signing New York outfielder Hector Lopez. When Arturo arrived in Japan he was told that he was going to be the starting third baseman. He said, "Fine, but there is one little problem. I'm left-handed." It turned out okay because Arturo was a speedy left-handed-hitting outfielder. He had the ability to hit pitches that weren't strikes. That was an asset in Japan with the big strike zone for foreign players.

One other thing that was very helpful to me my first year was that Wally Yonamine was a coach. Wally was one of the first foreign stars in Japan. He was second-generation Japanese from Hawaii. In fact, Wally had played pro football with the San Francisco 49ers, and then he went to Japan and became a star in baseball. He acted as my translator a lot of the time when I didn't know what was being said. He helped make things work out smoothly.

Our spring training was in Hawaii that year and I got off to a good start and was hitting balls all over the place. I made a good first impression with the long ball.

By going to Japan and playing well, I thought I would get noticed again after a year or so and a major league team would call me back. That's how I felt about going to Tacoma, too, and that didn't work out. The Cubs brought me back from Tacoma that time, but I didn't get a chance to play regularly. The pinch-hitting was like them saying, "The ship's sinking. Save us." That's when they stuck me in there one at-bat at a time.

George Altman

I have some good memories as a pinch-hitter. But I wasn't that comfortable with doing it because I didn't want to be doing it. I wanted to play every day. You can be a good pinch-hitter if you are a good first-ball, fastball hitter and you have a good attitude. That's what it takes. I was getting older and I didn't want to be just a pinch-hitter. I had three difficult years in a row with injuries and I wanted a last chance to play as a regular. I wasn't going to get it in Chicago, so I went to Japan. I had to face the fact that my time in the major leagues was probably over, at least temporarily. I was 34 in 1967, my last year with the Cubs, so I knew it was a long-shot to get back. I had to look at my situation as starting fresh in Japan. Especially back then, big league clubs were looking to replace you when you got to 34 or 35, so it wasn't likely I was going to get an offer to come back. However, I always wanted to play professional baseball until I was 40. That meant I should have a fairly long way to go—somewhere.

Some people thought I was depressed about leaving the majors, but I felt it was just a matter of not getting the opportunity I needed to play well again. It was more deflating that I felt I had missed out on opportunities and that seasons got away from me because of injuries. I felt that I should have had a better major league career. I suppose I could have taken better care of myself in terms of being out late at night on the road, getting more sleep, and things like that, conditioning and nutrition. But there wasn't the same emphasis on nutrition and training back then. If I had stayed in the hotel to go to sleep early, I might have been ostracized by my teammates for being anti-social.

So I signed on to play in Japan for the Toyko Orions and I joined the team for spring training in either late January or early February of 1968 in Hawaii. They did start early. Teams in Japan really believe in conditioning. In fact, the players are expected to start working out on their own in November. Nowadays players in the majors do train all year 'round and lift weights and run. Back then we had to work off-season jobs so when we came to spring training it really was to get in shape for the season. Now the big league players are already in shape when they report in late February or early March.

I actually fit in pretty well with the Japanese style. I liked working out. The first thing we did was calisthenics, running and stretching. A lot of it. It was stamina type stuff. And then we had hours and hours of working on fundamentals. We did a lot of hitting — I liked and needed a lot of batting practice. We did a lot of fielding drills, throwing to hit the cutoff man, infield training and practices where you learn where you're supposed to be on each kind of play. We did a lot of bunting, small things, what gets called small ball now.

There was a lot of repetition, a lot of time put into doing the same things over and over. I can't say I was surprised or put off by it. I didn't have any expectations as to what it would be like going in. I just went in with the attitude of whatever they come up with, I'm for it. I would do whatever they were doing. After all of my injuries, all of the muscle pulls and strains, I wanted a workout program that put me into better shape. I walked right into one, so it was good for me. Philosophically I was on board for this before I even knew it existed. Extra workouts, extra training, all fine with me. I was looking around at all of these players and they were all little guys compared to me at 6–4 and 200 pounds. I

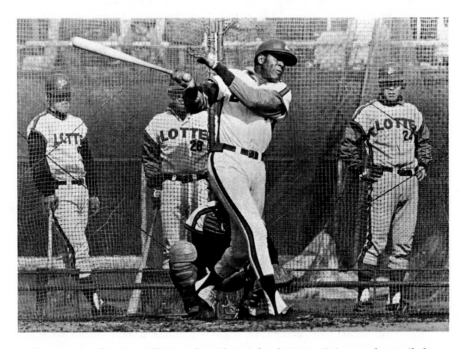

Altman was a five-time All-Star when playing for the Lotte Orions and compiled a lifetime average in Japan of over .300 while smacking more than 200 home runs.

figured if they could do it, I could do it. They were all under six feet tall. I was by far the tallest guy on the team.

The season in Japan stretches over about the same length of time as the season in the majors. We started around April 1 and ended in September. They play 144 games now, but we played 138. So we had a few more days off during the regular season than the majors did, which had expanded to 162 games in 1962. But we didn't get real days off. If there wasn't a game scheduled, we practiced. We hardly ever had a completely free day off during the season. It was just about a seven-days-a-week thing. Well, we had maybe one day off a month. If there was a rainout, you didn't just leave the clubhouse the way they do in the majors. We would practice indoors.

It was still baseball, but it was different than the majors. Not so different that I couldn't fit in. However, there were a lot of other adjustments that had to be made culturally and there was the language barrier. I didn't speak much Japanese. Transportation was interesting in Tokyo, too. The cab rides were an adventure. They were kamikaze drivers, very skillful, but scary. The other problem was that after games it was hard to catch a cab because the games would end at around the same time that the night clubs let out, so you were competing with those who wanted taxis at closing time. The night clubs had hundreds of girls working there who wanted rides home and I guess they were good tippers, so the drivers rushed to pick up the good-looking girls instead of foreign baseball players. I didn't know exactly what was going on all of the time, but there were plenty of times an American standing on the corner watched an empty cab go right by.

I had an apartment in Tokyo, but it was across town from the ballpark, several miles away. The plan was to catch a cab for the ride home, but it took so long sometimes that I had to find other means of transportation. I learned about the train and began taking the subway to get home. One of the other players, pitcher Massaki Koyama, lived near me and he would come by and pick me up and we would walk to the subway. That's how I learned how to get to the park and back home on the subway.

Our home night games started at about seven o'clock, but we got to the park about two o'clock, five hours before the game. As soon as we got to the park we would take about 30 minutes to practice, exercise and stretch, a warm-up. Then we took our pre-game batting practice. After that they had a meal for us, a small snack, really. We ate by ourselves after they gave us box lunches. My favorite food in the United States was hamburgers and cheeseburgers. That's what I was used to, and as a ballplayer who didn't pay much attention to his diet I ate a lot of them. But I'm not a fussy eater. I'm pretty diverse in my choices. I'm not difficult to please. It was fine whatever they gave us.

It was not cheeseburgers. Well, at least it was not the all-beef cheeseburger I was used to eating. Sometimes there were hamburgers and cheeseburgers available. You could find them to eat around Tokyo, but they weren't the genuine article. They were laced with something that was a bit fishy. There was fish meal or something in the burgers. Being able to get pure meat was just too expensive.

A typical boxed lunch for the pre-game snack had a pickled egg, rice, tofu and some kind of sardine-type fish. Other times we had curried rice. That was a big one. It was pretty good, though sometimes it was a little hot. I got used to their box lunches and I liked them. Sometimes I ran across a menu that had squid on it. That was kind of a stinky dish. Squid is definitely not on my list of favorite foods.

Road trips were definitely interesting, especially in some of the outer, farther away cities where they didn't have western-style hotels. Some American players had it in their contracts that they would always have a hotel room and didn't have to stay with their Japanese team. In some of the outlying areas where we played, the team stayed in these places that were not anything like Sheratons or a Marriot. Everyone slept on the floor on these mats. They were called tatami mats. They are very flat, kind of like sleeping bag pads, I guess. Also, the places we stayed in had no central heat. There was a little space heater and you'd burn up in the front and freeze in the back. We slept in yukatas, which are cotton robe type things, and wore footwear like sandals, without socks. We were freezing.

People have the idea that major leaguers open up cans of beer in the locker room after games, but I'll tell you there were no cans of Budweiser in the locker room in Japan. Sometimes everyone on the team would eat meals together, sitting all at one long table. The food was served from big pots with chicken or fish in it. It was like a stew and it was served with rice. Everybody would take their chopsticks out and dig in and pick up their stuff to eat. If there was anything left they would dump it back in the pot. My wife would have a fit over that type of communal meal. She couldn't stand people dipping in the pot with more than one serving spoon — that spoon must not touch anyone's plate, much less one's mouth.

Until I went to Japan I had never used chopsticks, never once even tried using them. It took some getting used to. I couldn't just ease into it, either. There were plenty of places I went where it wasn't a choice. There were no forks, so I had to use the chopsticks. I wasn't all that quick on the draw getting my food out of the pots with my chopsticks either, and by the time I got through fishing through it, a lot of the food was gone. I think I lost a little bit of weight from eating less. The other players showed me how to handle the chopsticks and after a while I got used to it and became a little bit more proficient. I got better, but didn't become an expert.

Most of my career in the majors my best playing weight was around 200 pounds. At times I gained some, but in Japan I dropped as low as 190 pounds once after I got sick. A lot of the time I was around 195 or 198 pounds. It had a lot to do with the size of the portions and what I ate. Out went those fatty hamburgers and cheeseburgers. There was a lot more rice and vegetables in my diet.

I mentioned freezing, but that was only in the beginning of the season. Once the summer arrived it was very hot and humid. One of the Japanese rituals was taking hot baths a lot. Between the heat and humidity, the baths, and the small portions served in restaurants, I had the tendency to lose weight. Americans going into restaurants are surprised at first when they see the size of the portions when they order a meal. It's like, "Where's the rest of it?" Sometimes the guys would order two meals at one time to get enough food. But after a while your stomach adjusts. Your stomach shrinks and you get used to eating smaller portions. When you get back to the States you are amazed at the large size of the portions served there.

I knew that a lot of things would be different in Japan and they were. I wasn't going to let the cultural differences bother me. It was educational and different. But I was there to play baseball and that was the most important thing to me. It was my opportunity to show what I could do at age 35 and show that I could still play.

16
"Pure Boru!" (Play Ball)

The team that George Altman represented in Japan was called the Tokyo Orions or the Tokyo Lotte Orions. Among the American players who competed in Japan while Altman was there were Army teammate Willie Kirkland, Dick Stuart, the former Pittsburgh Pirate, Jim Gentile, the onetime Baltimore Orioles slugger, and Lee Thomas, Altman's old teammate on the Cubs.

American players with credentials who wished to extend their playing careers were appreciated in Japan. While the connection to baseball did not prevent the United States and Japan from becoming enemies in World War II, there was evidence that baseball healed the wounds. When General Douglas MacArthur served as what was essentially the ruler of ruined Japan from 1945 to 1948, one way he encouraged understanding between American occupying troops and builders and Japanese citizens, was supporting regular participation in baseball.

Only two months after the countries signed a peace treaty, the occupying Americans sponsored a series of professional exhibition games and helped re-establish Japanese high school play in 1946. Lefty O'Doul, a magnificent hitter of the 1920s who batted .349 lifetime, left the majors for the AAA San Francisco Seals in 1934. In 1949, O'Doul led the Seals on a playing tour of Japan. He also brought massive quantities of baseball equipment to the country to jump-start the sport and played a role in major league teams visiting Japan in their off-seasons as well as in establishing the new post-war, professional league in Japan.

One of Altman's teammates in Tokyo for a time was former Dodgers second baseman Jim Lefebvre. They were on the club when a Japanese manager took over and tried to issue a blanket rule about running the bases. That manager wanted every player to slide head-first going into every base *in order to show the team's ownership his players were hustling. Head-first slides were frowned on in the United States because more injuries occur on those plays than in a typical, feet-first pop-up slide. Altman and Lefebvre refused to go along with that program.*

With everything tightly regulated, schedules locked in, and authority generally highly respected, all in the interests of conformity, Altman was surprised to learn that umpires— seen as law enforcement on the field in the U.S.— didn't seem to have the same clout in Japan when he was playing. Altman actually witnessed umpires being pushed or shoved on the diamond without the offender being punished by exile from the game or by being slapped with a large fine, as he would have been in the United States. Almost as surprising, Altman watched as a lengthy argument on the field might convince an umpire to change his call. That never happened in the United States. A protesting manager would be thrown out of a game for vociferous objections and the umpire would signal for play to resume.

Japan is a very ethnically homogeneous society, so anyone in public life who is not built like the average Japanese person or who does not look like the average Japanese person stands out. Altman stood out. He was African American, not Asian. And he was 6-foot-4 and towered over the majority of the people. This resulted in him being stared at a lot. The locals did more than stare at Altman when he went for a walk or to a restaurant.

"Fans would follow me around like a freak," Altman said.[17] After a while he got used to that level of attention and sloughed it off.

Tokyo was Altman's home base in Japan and the city, which had been ravaged by World War II but was rebuilt and thriving when it hosted the 1964 Summer Olympics, was a noisy, active crush of a place that was home to millions of people. Tokyo was the political, cultural and entertainment center of Japan. Baseball was the national sport.

Everything was great during spring training in Hawaii, nice weather and everything, and then as soon as we got back to Japan and began playing exhibition games in the cold weather I pulled a hamstring muscle. I couldn't believe it. Another injury. Not again. The first few weeks I was limited to pinch-hitting again.

I pinch-hit a three-run homer off of one of the top pitchers in the league. That ball traveled. It was a blast that seemed to hitch a ride on an airplane. I was told a lot of Americans hit an early home run like this where the ball travels completely out of the stadium, but as time goes on their long hits become shorter. You know why? It's because you have to take all of those hot baths. We used to see a new player come in and hit a shot that was downtown and we'd say, "Wait till the hot water hits him." It affected your strength, it seemed.

Another thing that happens to American players when they get to Japan is they realize they are not always competing on a level playing field. You are always going to be a foreigner, or gaijin. There was kind of a general mixed reaction from the Japanese to an American who came to their country to play ball. All of the major leaguers were supposed to be better than the Japanese players—that's why they were hired. Yet some of the Japanese players were jealous and wanted to prove they were as good as or better than the American players. There was also the very rigid set of rules that Japanese teams operated with. Some Americans that didn't believe in curfews or working out hard could never make it in Japan. They didn't stick around long. At the same time there was a lot of pressure on you to do well for a team since they were paying you this money to come from overseas, salaries that were larger than 90 percent of the Japanese players were making. There was an undercurrent of feeling among those that didn't want you to do well, and that didn't think any American players should interfere with Japan's national game. There was sort of a low-key conspiracy almost always in the works to make it harder for you to succeed. It drove some American players nuts and drove them right back home, but it was very real and you had to cope with it.

Growing up playing sports in the United States, you always have it ingrained in you that the rules are the same for everyone, that it's a level playing field for everyone. Well, in Japan it wasn't. The prejudice you saw could be overt. And I don't mean due to skin color. This was mostly because of nationality, for not being Japanese. The first and most obvious thing was the strike zone. Americans had a different strike zone than Japanese players. Balls and strikes could be anywhere, not just over the plate, not just between the waist and the shoulders.

Strikes were called on pitches that were way off the plate, inside, outside, up, down. Once, after a strike was called on a pitch that almost hit the ground, someone translated an umpire's comment for me. He said, "What are you complaining about? You like the low ball." The pitch was ankle high. I said something back to him like, "Yeah, I like ice cream, but I don't like the whole churn-full at once."

Things could get pretty extreme in terms of prejudice against American players. If an American was closing in on a record, there might be an unspoken pact made between teams to prevent him from reaching it. That might also apply to leading the league in a category. Fans wanted Americans to do well, but not too well, not at the expense of the name, the fame, or the records of Japanese players.

A Japanese player who was a big star was traded to our team. At the time I was leading the league in hitting, and he was put into the lineup in front of me. I was hitting .350 or .360 when he got to Tokyo. Time passes in the season and it's getting to be July or August. The team was right there in second place, closing in on first. We played this team and my teammate, who is a big, strong guy, but who hits a lot of grounders to right field, is catching up to me in the batting race. The other team puts on a fielding shift where they move the second baseman to the third-base side of the bag, meaning they have three infielders on the left. They pitched my teammate low and away the way he liked it, and he went four-for-four on ground balls to the right of second.

He was a big, lumbering guy, not a speedster on the bases, and every one of those times that he got a single on a grounder he tried to steal second and the other team threw him out. So they helped give him those four hits so he could catch me in the batting race, and he paid them back by getting thrown out trying to steal bases, so they weren't hurt. Against another team that did not put the shift on, our guy hit the ball to the second baseman. Their second baseman caught the ball and instead of throwing hard to first he made a balloon throw to first base so he could beat it out, though running at a slow pace. Their infielder cursed him out and said, "We're trying to get you a hit and you don't run." Yes, they did play those kinds of games with us. On another play, I hit a line shot that bounced over the shortstop's head. It almost decapitated him. It was over the shortstop's head, and he got called for an error to take the hit away from me.

Daryl Spencer had a very good career in Japan that started before I got there. He played there from 1964 to 1972. At one point in the earlier years he was chasing after the home run title. A pitcher on the Orions who was known to be a control artist and hadn't walked anybody in like 60 innings walked Spencer four times in a row. The third time he didn't even throw a pitch close to the plate. The fourth time Spencer came up in the game, instead of holding the bat by the handle he stood there holding the top of the bat. The pitcher still wouldn't pitch to him. He walked him again. That's what I mean when I say the prejudice against American players could be overt. The pitcher was Koyama, my teammate who showed me how to use the trains in Japan. He was a good guy, but felt he had to help keep a foreigner from winning the home run title.

I had heard about such things going on, but it was hard to believe. The foreign players talked about it amongst ourselves. One thing we knew was that any time we got a good pitch to hit we had to swing at it. You knew you might not see another one in that at-bat and maybe all day. Another adjustment I made was that I got a longer bat, like one of the old-time bats with a big handle that might weigh 40 ounces. It was pretty heavy with a long handle and it was cut so it didn't flare out. It was straight up and down, more like a pole. I used that for a while. It helped you on the outside pitches.

The strike zone could be a problem. You spend your entire career, your entire life, approaching hitting one way, and then the rules change on you. We had the American strike zone and the Japanese strike zone. The Japanese pitchers liked to throw a ball right up under your arm. The Japanese pitchers liked to pitch inside, off the plate to foreign players who had long arms, and right at our elbows. I had a habit of not moving much and just lifting my arms as the ball almost hit me. The umpire would yell, "Strike!" I'd say, "Wait a minute, that's not a strike." Then it would happen again. "Strike!" I remembered how Willie Mays used to handle inside pitches. When pitchers threw inside like that he used to hurl himself backwards very dramatically. So I did that, falling all of the way back. Umpires didn't want to lose face and if it looked to every-body in the stands as if I was almost hit by the pitch, it would make them look bad if they called the pitch a strike, as if they made a mistake. You know, the ball almost hit the guy. I started doing a little bit of acting to fight back against those pitches and I got the calls inside instead of the pitcher. It turned into a psychological game, but I had to make adjustments.

All of this was designed to prevent foreign players from winning batting titles and home run titles, or setting records. They thought that it was a bad reflection on their league if Americans who weren't playing in the majors anymore came over and could win hitting titles. The goal was to raise the perception of baseball in Japan as being the equivalent of the majors. There was a dream or aspiration for an international World Series. That's what was behind it. So they couldn't have these foreign players, particularly those of us who were seeking a second career, come over and do better than the best Japanese players. There were very few guys who had been stars in the major leagues who came over. If those of us who weren't really big stars in the United States came over and performed so well, it was a reflection on their league.

The longer you played in Japan the more you were accepted, but you were still never going to be one of them completely. One year I did actually win the RBI title, but most of the time I finished second or third, or something like that. One time I was leading the league in hitting, at about .356, but I got sick and didn't finish out the whole season, so I didn't qualify for the batting title. At various times I led the league in hitting for three weeks or a month, but never at the end of the year.

Overall, the caliber of baseball played in Japan was good. It was not as good as the major leagues. I would say there were definitely ballplayers of major league ability. But on average, and this was the reason the Americans were welcome to play, there was not enough high-quality depth. They didn't have enough great ballplayers. There might be a major league-caliber player at one position, but playing next to him in the field might be a player who would be Class B in the United States minors. The talent level was very spread out. Of course there were players like Sadaharu Oh, who would have done well in the major leagues.

There were some good pitchers, too. The best I saw was Yukata Enatsu of the Hanshin Tigers. He was a left-hander and he put on the greatest exhibition I've ever seen in an All-Star Game. He was a hard thrower with a real big curve. He pitched three innings and struck out all nine batters. Then he hit a home run, I believe a grand slam. That's as good as it gets in a baseball game.

I couldn't believe it when I got hurt right away in Japan, but the injury only held me back briefly. I became a regular and I started playing very well. I was glad to be there and playing baseball, and I enjoyed it

16. "Pure Boru" (Play Ball)

When George Altman (tall in center) left the United States to play professional baseball in Japan he joined the Tokyo Orions, which later became known as the Lotte Orions.

because it was different and interesting. My teammates were very, very good. My American teammate was Arturo Lopez, and we had a good time together.

Since we played or practiced every single day we didn't have much time to get out for tourism. But hanging out at the Western hotels, we saw a lot of great American entertainers who were playing Toyko. There were stateside entertainers like Dizzy Gillespie, Nancy Wilson and Wilson Pickett. We met them all. That was cool.

I think I hit .330 my first year in Japan. Once I was healthy, as I had long hoped, I did prove I could still play at a high level. That was very satisfying to be able to show that to people who felt I was washed up and should retire. I may have had the fleeting thought, "I can still play in the majors," but I did not believe it was going to happen.

In 1968, my first year in Japan, I was already 36. In the United States they were pushing guys out of the game at that age, not taking on guys who would be 37 by the next season. I felt the American teams in the majors wouldn't be paying attention to me at that age no matter what I did on the field in Japan. It seemed as if teams rushed guys out of the game at a younger age than they do now. So I didn't delude myself into believing that a major league team was going to call me, give me a contract, and play me full-time.

After one season in Japan I had fulfilled my main goal for going there. By staying healthy, except for the beginning of the season, I had proved I could still play the game. Going to Japan was interesting and fun, too. I knew I wasn't going to be able to play baseball forever, but I still didn't want to quit. I decided that I would keep playing in Japan for as long as I could play at a high level. If I had an off-season I was going to retire. I had no idea I would play in Japan for eight seasons. Most of the Americans stayed for no longer than two or three years. They passed through and I stuck around. There was always a close bond between the Americans that played together in Japan, even with the guys on opposing teams. We talked all of the time when we played against one another, and we exchanged stories about life in Japan and things that happened to us. The American players had the most in common with each other, and besides, we all spoke English.

When I left the United States to play in Japan it was a one-year, experimental commitment. I had enough fun and gained enough satisfaction that I ended up having almost a complete second career playing ball in Japan.

17

Being an American in Japan

One thing George Altman did to cope with the differences in daily life in Japan was to take notes. He did not keep a full-fledged diary of his experiences, but he wrote down information that provided tips for him or that he found interesting or amusing.

Inside one of his notebooks Altman folded a sheet of paper that served as a cheat sheet for measurements on clothing in case he wanted to go shopping. The form he wrote up told him the difference between measurements in inches and measurements in centimeters. It was not an all-encompassing chart, but rather offered hints within a range.

On Altman's chart a waist size of 94 centimeters equated to 37.01 inches and a waist size of 62 centimeters equated to 24.41 inches. Sleeve length of 76 centimeters matched 29.92 inches, and a length of 66 centimeters was 25.98 inches.

In another notebook Altman took note of his clothing needs. "Buy: Shoes, dress brown, boots black. Black short jacket leather, high class sport shirts (knit), 1 knit suit, 1 knit sport coat, shorts, undershorts, socks.

One of Altman's diaries offered insight into what it was like to show up for spring training at the end of January inside Japan.

Met team at Harada at 12 o'clock for flight to Kagoshima. We were met at airport by all-girl band and about 50 fans. We took bus to downtown Kagoshima. We had to take off our outer coats and hats and listen to the welcome address by the mayor at city hall outside in 40-degree weather. Later that night we had a reception at the Sun Royal Hotel. It was quite a success. The fans really turned out for this. They filled that huge reception room. It was SRO.

We filed on the stage one by one. The stage lights overhead were very bright. I remarked (to another player) that it was very hot. He said, "That's because you are so close to them. Us short fellows don't feel them so much." The reception consisted of the usual short speeches and singing by the rookies.

An ample supply of beer was placed on each table for the traditional "Compie." When someone offers to pour a drink for you, it's a token of friendship and should be accepted and the favor should be returned immediately. I had about seven or eight glasses in front of me at one time. I would sip from each glass offered even though I didn't drink too much that night.

We had a meeting after the reception. The meeting consisted mostly of going over our daily schedule.

The no-fooling-around schedule began with a wake-up call at 7:30 A.M., and the very busy day ended with an in-your-room curfew of 10:30 P.M. and lights out at 11 P.M.

Playing baseball in Japan wasn't weird, but it could be different, and that included the road trips. Once the Tokyo team was playing a series of exhibition games in a mountainous area and we were staying in a type of resort hotel. This was my first season when I was nursing that strained hamstring. The players were sitting around killing time by playing cards and I decided to help my injury by going down to the baths at the hotel. They had huge baths and whirlpools.

These were communal baths. The water was incredibly hot. I mean scalding. Whew! I figured that had to help loosen up the muscle. My teammates were all upstairs playing cards when I went down to the bath. Nobody else was using the water. The attendants give you a little towel that you use to uh, put in front of you. It was a sauna type thing I was going into in a way, but it was just hot water.

I went down to one end and I noticed that at the other end they had a nice view. I was in the water by myself and I left the little towel at the first end. I was down at the other side looking at the view and in comes a whole family. I don't have any clothes on at all. The father, the mother, the grandmother, a son and his wife and a couple of kids all come in to the baths and they get disrobed and enter the water. They weren't wearing any clothes either except for the little towel the size of a face cloth. They saw me, but they didn't pay any attention to me.

On top of everything else, to make it more embarrassing, I'd been in spring training for weeks without my wife so I got a little aroused down there. I wasn't about to get out of that pool and my towel was far away. I was trapped. I just stayed in the water at the far end. I'm not sure how long I was in the water, but it was at least 40 minutes. Finally, the family left. Man, my skin was like a prune. When I got upstairs, the

George Altman never envisioned having a long career in Japan, but he played professional ball for eight seasons on the island nation. One year the Tokyo team held spring training in Arizona. Altman is standing at right.

other players asked why I had been down there at the baths so long. I told them and boy, they jumped up and down laughing.

Another thing that I had a learning curve on at the communal baths was that you have to take a shower before you go in. When I first went to Japan I didn't know the rules. The Americans would just go over there and jump right into the baths. The Japanese people in the pool would look at you and then the workers would have to empty the whole pool to clean it. "Because of stupid gaijin," they'd say.

Gaijin referred to any foreigner, but there weren't many black people around. The only other black people I saw in Tokyo were other ballplayers, entertainers, and an occasional serviceman or two. Sometimes there were Latin and Korean foreign players in the league, too. I was already a minority in the United States, but I was really a minority in Japan. I don't think it mattered much that I was black. I think it mattered that you were a foreigner, black or white. We could learn something about how the Japanese stick together as a nation.

Japan was very much a closed society if you were a foreigner. That meant there were clubs you couldn't go into. You had to be Japanese. These were elaborate, fancy night clubs. When I first got to Japan and I wasn't playing much because of the hamstring, I think the club figured I was lonely and bored. A couple of club officials took me out with them to a club that had all of these beautiful girls there. It seemed as if there were hundreds of them. They were supposed to be entertainment hostesses. What they did was sit down with you and talk and make you feel like you were the king of the world. In the meantime, they were gleaning information about what you did and getting an idea if you were rich or not, and while that was going on the tab on the drinks kept growing. They got excited when I said I was a ballplayer. The average foreign business guy who goes over there isn't shy about saying that he's a vice president of a major company to get more attention from the girls. They were buying them drinks, and the more money the girls thought the businessmen had the more they got charged. That's how the girls made their money. I would wager that their drinks weren't as potent as the customers' either.

The bars' rate was what they called "charge by the face." That means you were charged as much as they thought you could afford. The foreign players learned that if we went out, and this was to the lesser clubs, not those elaborate clubs, to say that we were members of the U. S. Army, in the service. That should indicate to the girls that we didn't make so much money and the drinks would be cheaper.

The regular season ended in September and the Toyko Orions always did well, finishing first or second in our six-team league. They may have expanded or changed teams in recent years, just as the majors have done since I last played with the Cubs. There was a league championship and then a Japanese World Series. If we won we'd almost always end up playing the Yomiuri Giants, which was Sadaharu Oh's team. They used to say that three-quarters of all baseball fans in Japan were Giants fans, and I believe 80 percent of the umpires.

Oh was the dominant figure in the game, but because he was half–Japanese and half–Chinese in such a homogeneous culture he was not the favorite player throughout the country. The favorite son was Shigeo Nagashima. Nagashima was a third baseman who had a lifetime average of .305 in a long career, and he also had two long stretches as manager of the Giants. He was the golden boy and some of that was because he was considered "100 percent." That meant he was 100 percent Japanese.

Nagashima was a very good player. He was like a Ron Santo-type player. Oh and Nagashima played together, so the Giants had the big studs. The Tokyo Swallows had a great pitcher named Masaichi Kaneda. His parents were Korean, but he became a naturalized Japanese citizen. He is the only pitcher in Japan baseball history to win 400 games. He also struck out 4,490 batters. He was a big left-hander who later became a Toyko Giants star. Guys like Oh, Nagashima, who won five Most Valuable Player awards in the Central League, and Kaneda could play in any league.

When the season ended, the Orions made it clear they would like me to come back and play for them again the next year, which was the 1969 season. I was getting older and was going to be 36 that season, but they didn't care. Performance is what counts, right? It wasn't only performance in Japan. You still had to fit in, and after my first season I had proven that I could do that.

There really weren't too many Americans who succeeded in Japan long-term. There were a lot of good players who came over from the United States and they just didn't cut it. You had to have a certain temperament and the ability to roll with things even if they seemed outrageous, like the strike zone. Whew! You're talking about making it tough to hit. Ask Joe Pepitone and Dick Stuart about how hard that was. They were both power hitters. Pepitone had some good years with the Yankees and he was kind of a flamboyant guy. I'm sure his personality was perfect for Japanese baseball.

Dick Stuart had some really good years with the Pirates and he once hit 66 home runs for a team in the minors. He used to talk about that all of the time. He could be very funny. Stuart was on the Pirates' 1960 championship team and he made a couple of All-Star teams. For Stuart, it was all about hitting long home runs. He didn't pay too much attention to defense. When Stuart saw the way the umpires manipulated the strike zone, he couldn't handle it. He was a strong fellow and he hit some long balls, but he wasn't a disciplined hitter and that's what you had to be in Japan, especially when you couldn't count on the uniformity of balls and strikes being called.

Pepitone was one of the first big-league players to wear a hairpiece. He liked the night life and he had a lot of ability to hit, too. But just like Stuart he was tripped up by the strike zone thing. He didn't adapt to the way things worked in Japan. I think some guys came over from the United States with the idea that baseball in Japan was just a glorified minor league operation and that they were going to tear it up at the plate. But it didn't work out that way for everybody. They ended up being unhappy and their teams ended up being unhappy with them, and many left the country early before their season was over.

The bigger the name the player made for himself in the United States, the more money he could command when he came to Japan. The imports basically made more money than most of the guys on a team except for the stars, I'm sure, so it made sense that there would be resentment from the Japanese players if the American acted like a prima donna, or he didn't do a good job. I made between $50,000 and $60,000 in Japan, and that was a lot more money than I ever got paid for a season in the U.S.

When Jim Lefebvre came to Japan from the Dodgers, I think he got paid $80,000, and he didn't have nearly as good a season as I did. I had two good seasons and the Orions didn't want to pay me anywhere close to what Lefebvre was making. I don't know if he hit .230. When it came time for me to sign another contract, I had some problems with management. I didn't have anything against Jim, but I was a top producer and I wanted to get paid for what I did.

The team was going through managers all of the time, too, and I had to adjust to that. I think we had three managers in my first three years, or four years, in Japan. As soon as I got used to one of them and made an impression on him because I worked hard, he was gone, and I had to make the same impression on another manager.

The first manager I had with Tokyo was a nice, easy-going gentleman. He might have been too easy-going in a way. I remember a couple of times that he was walking up and down the dugout looking for a pinch-hitter. The pitcher on the other team was throwing aspirin tablets by us and was getting everyone out. He would look up and down the bench and tell a guy to get ready to pinch-hit and say, "Good, good, you go up to hit." The players are sitting there going, "No, thank you. No, thank you." They're telling him no, they don't want to go up to the plate. And he's letting them get away with it, looking for someone else to hit instead.

One thing I can tell you, Leo Durocher would have shipped that guy out in a heartbeat if a player ever tried that with him.

After my first season in Japan I was much more relaxed about the whole experience because I had been through it once. Every season is different, and things change when players change and the manager changes, but I was used to the big stuff.

My wife Rachel joined me in Japan and the environment was different. She was Hispanic but looked Caucasian, and we heard about that a lot in the United States, but not in Japan. That lifted some of the daily life pressure off us. She didn't like Japan that much, though, for a different reason. It was definitely a man's world in Japan, with the women subservient. It was a man's country and you would see things like the manager of the team on a road trip with his wife trailing behind him carrying the suitcases. My wife was not going to go for that. She wasn't going to be carrying my luggage and walking behind me.

Another thing was that a lot of booze was sold at the ballparks, and sometimes when the wives were sitting in the stands some of these crazier young Japanese fans tended to follow them and harass them. They would grab at the women. It was a much bigger problem at that time for women traveling on the subway, especially at the several times of day during business hours and rush hour when the cars were packed like sardines. The trains are so crowded that the transit system has the job of professional train packer. Those people go around and pack the people in as tight as possible. That was paradise for perverts and pickpocket specialists. It was a known fact that you didn't want to ride the train at the busiest periods.

Going on a road trip was different in Japan than in the majors. One of the things about the majors was that you would pack your suitcase for a trip and bring the bags to the ballpark when you had a getaway game. You turned them over to the club and you didn't worry about carrying them, and the next time you saw them was in your hotel at the new city you were playing in. Not in Japan. You had to bring all of your own bags and sometimes we had two-week road trips. You bring your own bat bag, too, so you might have four or five bags. I had never even seen a bat bag before.

So you have your bat bag, too, which is heavy, changes of clothes, and underwear. It was a major trip. I finally got all of the stuff into a cab and get to the train station and I'm looking for a redcap to help me out. What's a redcap? Right. Our first trip was to Osaka and I had to ask how to catch the train. The train station was huge and crowded and it looked as if there were a half-mile of steps to go up and you've got all these bags. Whew! I get all of this stuff carried up to the top like I was a pack mule. Arturo, my teammate, shows up in the same situation and we're in this massive crowd and we can't even get to the train. We missed that train. Then along come some veteran teammates and they're only carrying light bags.

I later learned why they didn't have to bring so many changes of clothes. They lived in a typical Japanese inn and were given yukatas—light cotton robes—to wear during their stay. They wore them practically the whole trip. Most of the time they didn't leave the inn except to go to the ballpark, so they never had to put on their street clothes until it was time to head to the game. I figured out that I didn't have to bring so many changes of clothes. I got a handle on the packing and cut way down the on the bags whenever we went somewhere. I learned fast.

18

Japanese Workouts
and Meetings

*A couple of things George Altman learned early about Japanese base-
ball were that the teams held more meetings in a week than a House of
Representatives committee would hold during a year, and that the workouts
to stay in condition started the moment spring training did and never eased
up during the season.*

*One year in one of his little black notebooks, Altman kept track of how
he fared when conditioning work began.*

January 2. The first two workouts were very hard, but brisk. We
were finished by 3 P.M. both days. The manager informed me that I
should go at my own pace, but do as much as I could. Well, my pace was
the same as theirs both days despite the fact that they had a two-week
start on me.

January 3. I found out I wasn't "him." Though I had been keeping
up with the young bloods for two tough days and knew my legs were
tired, I felt real optimistic today. The manager had been calling me
"Superman" for two days. I felt so good I was inclined to believe him. I
was great in the long-distance running, but they threw me in the dashes
for the first time. That's when I found out I wasn't Superman, nor his
close relative. I was conservative on the first two dashes and came in last
both times. One of our trainers was in the group with me. Now he is
about 4-foot-2 and was running away from me each time. The kids in
the stands kept yelling to me to do my best and good luck. That made
me feel a little ashamed and I decided to go all-out for the third race.
Well, I won the race, but found out I wasn't Superman. My permanent

groin trouble surfaced after I crossed the finish line in victory. Superman doesn't wilt at the first demanding test.

January 5. I came down to dinner after a short, but hard workout. It rained and we had our first bout with the track. Here we pray that it doesn't rain, for when it does they take us over to the track for some marathon running. Today we did three miles, and then went to the diamond for our practice. When I came down to dinner they were serving a cocktail of turtle blood. My stomach wasn't feeling up to it and I passed. Most of the players, including Jim Lefebvre, downed it with no sweat.

January 6. Today was cold and rainy so we went back to the track. We did over five miles in 40 minutes. The turtle blood must have been working for only Jim dropped out, and he went about 17 laps. My leg was hurting, but it was important to me to stay with them.

I heard that Frank Howard, the big first baseman who used to play with the Los Angeles Dodgers and Washington Senators, had his first practice in Japan today. (Frank was such a big guy at 6-foot-8 and about 260 pounds that his nickname was "The Washington Monument." He reportedly took 30 swings and hit 15 for home runs, with two of them going out of the stadium. Last night I was asked if Frank was the biggest player in the major leagues last year. I answered that he is the biggest player in the world.

Jim Lefebvre and I started playing chess today. We talked about it all year last year, but never played. I think it's great for developing concentration, which is the most important part of hitting. In 1961, when I had my best year in the majors, I played a lot of chess. Mental exercise may be just as beneficial as physical training.

January 8. A day off. Jim and I went to the movies. It was very cold and windy, a good day to be off. When we came out of the movie, it started to snow. Snow in Kagoshima, the Florida of Japan!

January 9. A very cold day! The one hour of exercise and running seemed harder today because of the bitter cold. It is days like today when the muscles rebel and begin to holler early that thoughts of retirement come up. I start to think maybe I'm one year late on that score.

February 19. Yesterday was an off day. The married players and others that wanted to were given permission to return to Tokyo to see their families. In America the players are allowed to bring their families to spring training. Here they are not allowed to do so, therefore the manager allows the players to return and spend a day with their loved ones. He believes it is good for team morale. They got back about 11 A.M. and reported for practice around 1 P.M. We had a relatively light practice today.

February 20. PAYDAY! We had a fast-paced morning walk which was an omen as to what to expect at the practice field. We started off by jogging 20 laps around the field. We were scheduled to do 15 wind sprints across the outfield, jogging back after each all-out sprint. We were obviously dragging by the eighth sprint, so the manager cut the sprints short. We were all perspiration-soaked after the one-hour "warm-up" drills. We were told earlier to bring an extra uniform. Believe me, we really need the extra. While we were changing uniforms, naturally the talk was of the severity of the practice. I found that even though the players grumble about how tough it is, there is a certain amount of pride about the team's fitness and the hard practice routine. We have to be one of the best-conditioned baseball teams in the world. The new players with the club also fall in with everyone else. They begin to make the inevitable comparison between last year's practice and this year's. They even begin to talk disparagingly about last year's training. I think that we may have overdone it a bit, but it's good in that it gives us an edge over the opposition. That is, if it isn't pursued to the point of no return. We will be in top condition when camp breaks. Therefore we should leave this type of training here.

February 21. My legs feel pretty good in the morning after I get loose despite the fact that I suffer from chronic left groin soreness. After we stop our continuous running routines, the groin stiffens and I have trouble moving around. However, when it is loose during sprints I have been running away from most of the players. In fact, I haven't lost a challenge yet.

Michiyo Arito, our third baseman, is generally regarded as the fastest player on the team, and I've beaten him twice. The players are amazed at my speed at 41. I must admit I'm a few months ahead of myself. It's usually June or July before I'm able to move at top speed. I'm hopeful that it's a dividend from my attendance at the Nassan Health Clinic this October. The doctor said I would be stronger, my reflexes improved, and the results would be good. So far I haven't been as sore and stiff after practices and my recovery period seems to be shorter. I don't feel as strong at the bat, but that may be due to the strenuous and tiring pre-batting drills.

Today I found out that we have a player who is allergic to a baseball glove. He has a terrible rash on both hands. The doctors told me that he should be in another business.

February 24. Rain began to fall as we started our warm-up exercises. The schedule was changed from regular practice to "Operation burn-out." We exercised and ran sprints for one hour. When we finished we were completely burnt out. Fortunately, the rain came down a bit harder near the end of the hour and we were excused for the day.

Tonight we had a meeting. I was surprised to find a lecturer from an insurance company addressing the team. Other guys thought he was selling insurance. However, it seems he was lecturing on performance production.

There was camaraderie between the American players on Japanese teams. There were only two foreigners on each team and almost all of them were American, so that meant there were only 24 American players at most in the country at one time. Some of the players I knew before from different places, and all of us had some things in common.

Willie Kirkland and I went way back to before we were even in the majors as Army ball teammates, and he was in Japan when I was. Marty Keough, Lee Thomas and Frank Howard played in Japan when I did. Fred Valentine, whom I played college ball with, was there, too.

Once Frank Howard came over he was hugely popular in Japan, not just huge. He hit a lot of home runs and he was a curiosity because he was such a big guy. People stared at me because I was tall and black, I guess, but Frank was a good four inches taller than me and outweighed me by about 60 pounds. I towered over almost all of the Japanese people I met, so you can imagine what kind of impression Frank made. I always felt that 1,000 eyes were following me when I was walking down the street. Maybe it was 10,000 sets of eyes for Frank. He was a big dude.

Pitchers didn't want to throw to him, and they seemed to have the umpires on their side calling balls and strikes. The pitchers were throwing off the plate and they were getting strikes from the umpires. They called that "hitting the heavy corner." The heavy corner meant that they were throwing two or three inches off the plate. There was a guy on our ball club who had electric stuff. He was a hard thrower with a great slider. But instead of trying to blow the ball past people he was trying to throw to the heavy corner. He rarely got to pitch. I asked one of the veteran pitchers, "Why throw to the heavy corner? Why aren't you pitching to this guy?" The guy said, "No. Heavy corner." I said, "You don't need the heavy corner with the stuff you have. You can throw it right down the pike and they'll probably never hit it."

Most guys weren't like me, staying and playing eight years. Daryl Spencer played for a long time. Dave Roberts stayed there for six years. This was the Dave Roberts who came up through the Pirates organization when the great Willie Stargell was the Pirates' first baseman. Roberts was a first baseman and he couldn't get to play except for very short periods. He came to Japan in 1967 and became the first gaijin to hit 40 home runs in a season. He played in Japan through 1973. The interesting thing was that there was another Dave Roberts who came along later who played in the majors, who actually was born in Japan, the son of a U.S. Marine, but he didn't play professional ball in Japan.

There was a player in Japan who played with me in the States named Lou Jackson. He was a great hitter in the Cubs organization in the minors, but he never made it with the Cubs and they traded him to the Orioles. But in 1966 he came to Japan. He had the makings of a great hitter. He was a little guy, but he had tremendous power. He could run, he could throw, and it seemed as if he could do it all. He actually died in Japan when he was only 33. I think too much booze contributed. He couldn't stay out of the bars. In 1967 he collapsed at the plate while he was playing for the Sankei Atoms. He died the next year from inflammation of the pancreas.

People that I knew and people in the baseball world were surprised when I first went off to Japan to play ball. They never expected that I would keep going back for years and years. But they didn't forget me, either. I maintained a home in Chicago and I worked for the Chicago Board of Trade during the off-season. Baseball writers always seemed to look me up when I was back in the States and ask about my Japanese baseball experiences. Stories would appear in the Chicago newspapers and *The Sporting News.*

One thing that they always laughed at when I told them was the game's terminology in Japanese. It was obvious that the words that were part of the game in Japan came from English. There may have been a language barrier for a lot of things, but a lot of the phrases used sounded very similar to what we used in the United States. The sport was called "beisu boro," so anyone could figure out that meant baseball. An out was "outo." No mystery in that word, either. The word in Japan for hit was "hitto."

People in the United States could never get over the stories I told about the umpires and the strike zone, and they really couldn't believe it when I told them that sometimes the umpires changed their minds. Once during a game there was an hour delay because the umpires debated a call on the field. The call was over whether or not one of our Orion base runners was guilty of interference. The decision switched back and forth a couple of times before we started playing again.

Sometimes the umpire made calls and the managers disagreed, and they wouldn't go along with it. In the U.S. there might be a five-minute delay, the managers would have their say, go back to the dugout, or get thrown out, and that was it. In Japan if the managers complained, all of the umpires would huddle for a meeting. Often they would change the decision. Then the other manager came out to plead his case like they were in court because now he wouldn't accept the decision. The umpires would huddle up again and change it back. It went back and forth like that for a long time until the managers finally got together and said okay. It was really strange.

The players were also known to push the umpires around a bit and get away with it. I remember once Shigeo Nagashima, the great hitter for the Yomiuri Giants, was called out on a third strike and Nagashima goes, "Oh, no, no, no. That's not a strike. Not a strike. That's a ball." And he refused to leave the batter's box. Instead of throwing him out of the game, the home-plate umpire called all of the umpires together and they had a meeting. Then he came back to the plate and said, "Mr. Nagashima, I'm sorry. You're out. You must accept the decision." All of the umpires agreed. Finally, I guess Nagashina felt he was overmatched and figured he'd better accept the strikeout. The umpires won that one.

One year we took spring training in Phoenix, Arizona, which meant that we had some exhibitions against the Major League teams that also trained there. We saw the Giants, the Oakland Athletics, and the San Diego Padres. There was a well-known sports columnist out of the Bay

Area and he wrote about me that season in a very complimentary way. He described me in a story as "tall, black, handsome and as suave as anyone who ever got a master's degree from Tennessee State ought to be."[18] The only non-controversial part of that statement was that I was tall and black. I never finished the work on my master's.

He also noticed the difference in how injuries were viewed. Of course I had one of my muscle pulls at the time and my thigh was taped as I sat out a workout and talked to him. The manager walked by and said, "Ah, Altman-san, you will be able to play tomorrow against Oakland. You play tomorrow. You be all right. You will be much better. You play."[19] That was one of my same-old early-season muscle problems and I can't remember whether I sat out the next day or not, but I did tell the writer that the Japanese teams don't like you sitting around doing nothing.

I also mentioned one of the peculiarities of Japanese baseball that drove me half-crazy. The team wanted every single throw from the outfield to go to the cutoff man. They didn't ever want you to throw to the plate. For them it wasn't a judgment call, but a rule. I disagreed, but I went along with it.

Although I saw some strange goings on in the way that foreign players were treated with the strike zone, and how everyone ganged up on a player doing too well, overall everyone treated me quite well and the fans were great when it came to their favorite players. They were great baseball fans and they idolized the best Japanese ballplayers, but they didn't do that much cheering for foreign players. I had the sense that they were cheering for their team as a whole and yes, for certain star Japanese players, but their allegiance to foreign players was less certain. The fans made a lot of noise, banging on drums and cheering, and they had special cheering sections, but I didn't really follow who the noise was for. You're trying to concentrate on the game. One thing that was pretty interesting was that when you had a good game or hit a big home run, they gave you prizes. It was like passing the hat in the low minors, or in the old Negro Leagues when they barnstormed.

Every time you had a big hitting game or had the game-winning hit or something, you might be given coupons for the grocery store, gift certificates for restaurants, toys and games for your kids and family. There were some food prizes, too, like noodles. I might hit a home run and get some noodles. They gave it to me at the end of the game. I won a lot of those prizes. They were all small prizes. They weren't giving you a bonus like a car or anything. I gave away a lot of that stuff to neighbors and teammates.

The first time it happened, when someone from the team came around and gave me one of those prizes after the game, I was surprised. I didn't expect it. Some of them were pretty neat prizes, too, especially the things for the kids. A lot of them involved electronics. Come to think of it, some of the prizes were cash. You might earn 5,000 yen. That sounded like a lot, but at that time I think the yen was 360 to the dollar, so it wasn't quite as much as you thought. It was only a little bit more than $13.

One year in the 1970s my contract was for 19,200,000 yen. It sounded like I was rich, but it definitely wasn't for $19 million like Albert Pujols gets. But I was making over $50,000 and that was a lot more than I ever made playing in the majors. I think the most I got was $65,000. That was really good because my living expenses were paid in Japan and $30,000 of that was exempt from U.S. taxes, I think. You know, the team paid the taxes for you, too, if I recall. That was 40 years ago. We got all sorts of discounts for playing on the team. At one time I had it in my contract that I got a bonus for hitting a certain number of home runs, but they also had it in there that if I didn't reach a certain minimum number of home runs I would be docked for it. I don't think the toy prizes factored into that.

I probably won a lot of prizes during the 1972 season when I hit 21 home runs with 90 RBI and a .328 average. It was just such a great feeling to know that I could produce like that when I was healthy, even at an advanced athletic age.

The longer I played in Japan the better I seemed to get, even though I was aging and had passed 40. That was my old goal, to play until I was 40. I had said I was going to keep playing in Japan as long as I kept playing well, but I was going to retire if I felt my skills were eroding. That never happened. Even my last year there with the Orions I was hitting better than ever, over .350, when I got sick.

I was several years into my involvement with Japanese baseball when I saw that San Francisco area writer in spring training, and I appreciated still being able to play the game. I told him, "I don't say that Japanese baseball is perfect. But it beats being a has-been over here."[20]

19

Nearing the End in Tokyo

At the front of one of George Altman's notebooks from his days of playing baseball in Japan, he wrote "1973 Goals." He said that he wanted to hit 30 home runs, drive in 100 runs, and bat .300. Those are the numbers of an All-Star and they work fine in the majors as well as Japan. That season his actual totals were 27 home runs, 80 runs batted in and a .307 average. He did not fare poorly as a prognosticator.

This particular notebook of Altman's was not so much a diary of happenings as it was a pitching memo charting the tendencies of opposing pitchers. He began his notations on the first day of the 1973 season.

Opening Day
Saturday, April 14th
Lions 8, O's 7.
Kato
1st — Shoots away-curve, then change-up away. 2nd — Shoots away (ball), umpire strike, change-up away, fast high (ball), change in; 3rd — Fast and change away — hit shot to second on fast away, 0 for 3.
April 19th
Flyers 2, O's 1.
Tatahashi
1st time up
Fast in (ball), shoots away, shoots away, 2nd, shoots away (ball) fast in. 1 for 2.
Suiganara, rh, shoots away (ball), curve and forkball, two strikes fast in 0–1.
Kaneda, Fast away (ball), change-up away and forkball, two strikes fast in, 1–1.
Tot: 2 for 4. Series Tot. 4 for 11, .363, 1 HR, 2 RBIs.

Altman documented months of games that way in small print, keeping track of what pitchers threw him. The notebook's contents were almost exclu-

157

sively sets of numbers and abbreviated pitching descriptions. Only rarely did he describe a pitcher in prose, and then only a few words. It must have paid off since on Easter Sunday Altman drove in six runs highlighted by a grand slam.

About as elaborate as Altman got in this collection of notations was when he wrote, "I didn't play (sore knee)."

However, smack in the middle of the notebook he jotted down some advice to himself and gave himself a pep talk.

1. Know pitchers; 2. Take care of body; 3. Wait. Get good pitch; 4. Concentrate; 5. Watch the ball all the way; 6. Be cheerful — happy; 7. Everything is beautiful.

Experiment — Don't be afraid of temporary failure. Know that with ingenuity and experience the strong will find a way to succeed. I can do it! I will do it!

Near the back of the notebook, Altman took note of unusual things that happened with the Orions during the 1974 season. Early in the year, still in April, the team had a scheduled television appearance and was hanging out in the waiting room.

Before the show about eight of us were sitting in the dressing room where we were served hot Japanese green tea. It was very quiet in there as the young girl passed out the tea. Most of the fellows seemed a bit nervous. All of a sudden Arito let out a deafening scream. It seemed that the young girl tipped her tray a bit and spilled some of the tea on his lap just as she was going out of the door.

That incident seemed tame compared to an April 28 brawl Altman described between the Orions and a team he didn't even mention. It seems as if The Ring *magazine founder Nat Fleischer would have loved being there.*

Hirota was coming in to score on a sacrifice fly to left when Miyandera stuck his knee out and it caught Hirota on the thigh. Miyandera did not have the ball when he stuck his knee out. Kaneda charged down from first and kicked Miyandera on the upper thigh. Don Buford (the old Orioles' player) who was playing third, jumped Kaneda from behind and the rhubarb was on. Bodies were everywhere, but mostly in one big pile near home plate. Players were kicking at each other with their spikes. Miyandera emerged with cuts inside his mouth and on his legs.

When order was finally restored, he was yelling "Negro" at Buford. At first I didn't know he was talking to Buford. I thought he was calling his pitching coach Neguro. He later apologized to me. I wasn't upset. There are a lot of other things he could have called him. The umpires threw Buford and Kaneda out of the game.

In June, a player named Bobby Williams gave Altman a book to read called The Power of Your Subconscious Mind. He read it and "from June 13 I have hit in four consecutive games. I believe in the power of the subconscious mind, faith and prayer."

A little bit later in June, the Orions got word that "a young girl hanged herself at the Plaza, the hotel that we stay in when we play in the Osaka area. The manager said we should change hotels. I don't think I will."

On June 25, Altman tied a Japanese league record by hitting a home run in his sixth straight game.

When I went to spring training in 1973 the new manager, Masaichi Kaneda, had upped the ante. As challenging as the workouts had always been, he made it almost twice as hard as before. The workouts were already rigorous, but he planned longer sessions. We'd get up early in the morning and run before breakfast. Then we would do two-a-day workouts. Sometimes we ran five miles before training. It was just at a ridiculous level actually. I was 41. I exceeded my expectations. I kept saying if I had a bad year I'd hang it up, but I just kept having good years so I stayed. I was making the Japanese All-Star team almost every year and I had a lifetime batting average of .309. I made a lot of All-Star teams, so they weren't keeping me off because I was an American. I can't remember what went into the selection, if fans voted, or sportswriters, or players. It seemed they went mostly by statistics. Making the All-Star team was a pretty big honor for me. Not a lot of Americans made the All-Star team in Japan. I know Daryl Spencer did, but there weren't a lot of U.S. ballplayers in those All-Star games in those days of collusion to keep the foreign players from the top levels of achievement. But then I can't remember if I felt others deserved to be on the teams that were left out.

By 1974 the umps seemed to ease up and in the late 1970s and 1980s the foreigners began to compete for and win individual titles. Randy Bass, the former Minnesota Twin, even won the Triple Crown in the Central League, the league of Oh and Nagashima. No way would that have happened a few years earlier.

When you were chosen for something that was discretionary, that meant that they liked you. It was a pretty good feeling. The Japanese used to give me a lot of respect and look at me as a gentleman. Somebody told me they thought I was a minister or something. I don't know how that got out. It wasn't true. I got along with everybody there, though. Some players who came from the United States didn't. I think Joe Pepitone lasted only 14 games before he left. He just wasn't the right fit for Japan. I showed a lot of respect for their culture. It was their country, their way of doing things, and it was my job to fit in. Nobody was going to adjust to me or to other Americans.

During my career in Japan I hit more than 200 home runs, too. Those were pretty good numbers, especially considering the circumstances and the way they cheated against Americans. Overall, though, what I did in Japan made me feel better about my baseball career and what I accomplished. I think I would always have been disappointed if I had retired after playing in the majors and the way those last few seasons went. This way I got to prove I was a better player than other people may have thought I was.

My time in Japan proved me right about what I had been thinking. If I stayed healthy I could have had some good numbers in the States. I had done it everywhere else I played. That was very satisfying.

When I returned to Chicago each year in the off-season some people wondered where I had been, but there were enough articles in the papers about me that a lot of sports fans knew what I was doing. The year we had spring training in Arizona, the writers were interested in me. I was one of only three people with the Orions who spoke a significant amount of English, so that made me an easier interview, too. At times over the years when I was playing well in Japan it did cross my mind that I could have been still playing in the majors. But I wasn't going to ask anybody for a job or put out feelers. If they wanted me, they knew where to find me. Nobody did, no matter what I was hitting.

When Willie Kirkland came over to Japan after his time in the majors, he joined the Hanshin Tigers. We talked a lot about life in Japan and I gave him some tips as a veteran of living in Japan. We played them in some exhibitions and it seemed as if every time I played against Willie I had a great game. He must have been a bellwether for me. One spring exhibition game I even remember going five-for-five and him running past me on the field saying, "Big Boy, you better save some of those hits for the season." It was just like playing with him on the San Francisco Giants again. Willie did okay in Japan. He hit a lot of home runs, but he didn't hit for average. He was a good defensive player and because he hit home runs he was popular in Japan.

I was in Japan long enough to pick up on some of the customs. After a while I began bowing when I greeted someone. When you were entering or leaving a place, you were expected to acknowledge the people, even if it was just with a phrase. You learned that when someone said "ah, so" it was a break in the conversation or to acknowledge that he was paying attention. In the United States when people are talking you just listen. The other guy has to discern whether you are paying attention or not. By saying "ah, so" you are telling the other person you are listening.

Joe Christopher, my teammate on the 1964 New York Mets, was the only person I knew who did that. Joe would repeat a word or two from your sentence. If you said, "I'm going to Chicago tomorrow," he would say, "Chicago tomorrow" while bowing his head. I think that was one of the reasons why everyone liked Joe so much — because he let you know he was paying attention to what you were saying.

It helped me a lot that we spent a lot of time staying in western hotels where a lot of people spoke English. The only time the team stayed at a Japanese inn was when we were playing exhibition games in the spring far from Tokyo.

One of the things that impressed me the most about Japan was the fact that the people were so courteous. Everything is so crowded, especially in Tokyo, and you end up standing in lines a lot. In other parts of the world the people might be pushy and grumpy in the same circumstances. But in Japan the people were courteous. I learned to be patient. Any time people bumped into you they said, "Excuse me." People seemed to respect each other there. There was hardly any crime, either. You could walk the streets at night, very late at night, no problem.

Sometimes my picture got into the newspapers and there were articles in Japanese where I was in the game story and things like that, but I couldn't read them. I had to have a friend act as an interpreter to tell me what they wrote about me. I saved some of the papers and the headlines are gigantic. I couldn't tell you what they say now. I never learned to read much Japanese, but I could recognize my name.

There is no doubt that Sadaharu Oh was a great player and that the whole country was enthralled by him. The first time I saw him play was on television. Every one of the Giants' games was televised because the team was so popular. Oh was not physically very big. He was about 5-foot-11 and fairly good-sized in his build, but not super powerful looking. He was a left-handed batter and he raised his front foot like Mel Ott did. He hit his 868 home runs and he hit them everywhere. He had power to every field, but he hit more home runs to right field. He was a good contact hitter. He was not a brute power hitter. The way he relied on his back foot keeping his weight back helped him hit some long home runs. He played in the other league and we mostly played against the Yomiuri Giants in exhibition games. One year, though, we met them in the Japan World Series.

In the first game of the Series I got walked four times. They wouldn't even come close to pitching to me. They brought in a left-handed pitcher and he didn't throw me strikes either. They brought in a right-handed pitcher and he didn't throw me strikes. They didn't want me to hit a home run. They didn't want the foreigner to look too good. I didn't hit too well in that Series because I became impatient and started swinging at bad pitches.

Mostly I saw Oh play on TV, wearing out teams on TV. In Oh's best year he hit 55 home runs, and he led the Central League in homers 15 times. He also won five batting titles. A couple of times foreign players made a run at the 55 homers, but they ran into the problem of Japanese baseball people not wanting to see the record go to anyone else. The first time it happened was 1984 when American Randy Bass had 54 home runs for the Hanshin Tigers going into the last game of the season, but the opposition intentionally walked him four times. In 2001, another American player, Tuffy Rhodes, hit 55 home runs and at the end of the year he was walked every time up. A third time, in 2003, a guy from Venezuela named Alex Cabrera had 55 home runs with five games left in the season. To round out the year, he was playing against the team Oh was managing. Oh ordered his pitchers to throw strikes to Cabrera, but they disobeyed him and walked him.

In November of 1974, there was a home run hitting exhibition in Japan between Hank Aaron, who had just broken Babe Ruth's career record, and Oh. I remember going to see that. I met Oh. He was a nice guy. I never talked hitting with him or anything like that, though. Aaron won the home run derby, but by just a few. They held it at the home park of the Yomiuri Giants. They had a huge crowd. It was pretty cool bringing those two guys together. It was kind of fun to see. Aaron ended up with 755 home runs and Oh ended up with 868. That was a lot of home runs on one field.

Oh and Shigeo Nagashima, the top players in Japanese ball, were on the same team and that's why the Yomiuri Giants were so popular. The Hanshin Tigers represented the Osaka area and they had a huge rivalry. Osaka was also the site of a national high school baseball tournament every year, and they would have 60,000 or more fans there for that tournament. Wow, 60,000 or more fans for a high school baseball game!

Even many years ago when I was playing in Japan, there were some great players who would have fit right in with the majors. I always felt that someday there would be more Japanese players who would come along and end up playing in the United States the way Ichiro Suzuki did and become a big star. I believed that if the players got bigger and stronger they would be candidates to play in the U.S. I didn't know how nutritional habits would change or help, but I knew the Japanese players would be good because they worked so hard at the game, they had the fundamentals and they observed. The last few years I was there, the third baseman for the Orions was Michiyo Arito. He was around 6-foot-1 or so. He was big enough. He looked like he could play major league ball. He was a good fielder with good speed and power.

There were other guys playing when I did besides Oh who could really hit. I wasn't surprised as the years passed and some Japanese players gave it a try in the states. More and more of them are doing it and making it, although an Ichiro doesn't come along every day in whatever country you're in.

I honestly did not know how long I would keep playing in Japan. Compared to the days in the majors my body felt good, even though I was getting up into athletic old age. I played a lot of racquetball in Chicago during the winters to stay in shape. I spent about five months out of the year in Chicago and the other seven in Japan. I was thinking of what I would do next, but I kept having good years in Japan and making the All-Star team, so why retire? I was still hitting .300 and the team kept giving me raises. I had set the goal of playing until I was 40, but I went beyond that.

When I first went to Japan I found out I could become a permanent resident if I stayed there 18 months straight, but I chose to split my time between the United States and Japan during my entire playing career there. I remained a U.S. resident.

Before my last season in Japan, the Orions were sold to a new owner. The old owner was a wealthy man in the motion-picture business in Tokyo and he called the team the Tokyo Orions. He sold the team to the owner of a company that sold undergarments, candy and gum. He changed the name of the team to the Lotte Orions. Lotte was the name of the company. But it was the same team.

Also near the end of my time playing in Japan — 1972 — we played an exhibition series against the San Francisco Giants in Hawaii. Honolulu was like halfway between Tokyo and San Francisco. The occasion was the 25th anniversary of post–World War II baseball in Japan. For me it was kind of fun playing against an American team. Willie Mays was still with them, and Willie McCovey. I always hit well against the Giants, too. And I still did during that series.

20

Health Scare
and Retirement

*George Altman knew he was coming to the end of the line in his base-
ball career. He considered any games he played beyond the age of 40 to be
icing on the cake, a bonus gift since by that age more than 90 percent of all
baseball players are retired.*

*He was lucky that he was able to keep playing beyond that birthday
that serves as a demarcation line for middle age, that he had a team that
still wanted him, and that he was still playing at an All-Star level. Never
once did he underestimate his good fortune on that front. It almost seemed
as if it were payback for all the difficulties he had earlier in his career with
pulled muscles and other injuries that limited his major league effective-
ness.*

*As someone with a college degree, Altman had never counted solely
on being a professional athlete for his adult life and had always tried to
prepare for life after retirement. He was certain it was going to be in
the financial world, but he just didn't know when his second career would
begin.*

*Even as the calendar slid into the mid–1970s and Altman approached
his 43rd birthday, he was still a first-rate addition to the Lotte Orions,
still a .300 hitter. He sometimes had hot streaks that brought his average up to the .350 area when he might lead the Pacific League for a little
while.*

*Ultimately, Altman's retirement from playing professional baseball
stemmed from his body letting him down — not by slowing his swing down,
but by illness. When Altman retired from Japanese baseball in 1976 it was
because he faced a life-threatening situation. Sickness cut short his 1974*

season and weakened his body to the point that it affected his 1975 per-
formance.

During my last year in Japan I was hitting really, really well for average and power. Really, I was swinging as good or better than ever. But
then I got sick. I began having stomach problems and internal bleeding.
One time I hit home runs in five straight games and another time I hit
seven home runs in five games. But I didn't feel well.

One of my old friends, Charley Pride, came to Tokyo during that
time period. Charley was a very good pitcher in the Negro Leagues and
probably would have made it to the majors if he hadn't hurt his arm. Of
course, then he turned to country singing and became famous doing
that. Charley came to Japan to perform and we had a fun reunion at the
hotel where he was staying.

I gave him a ticket to the ballgame and he went to the game that
night. But that day I had spent hours getting tests at the hospital. I wasn't
able to eat or drink anything and I was in a weakened state. We were
playing against Osaka and they had a left-hander named Suzuki that I
didn't hit well anyway. He was the Sandy Koufax of our league. He was
tough. But the series right after that we went to Osaka and in another
game against the same pitcher I got a single and was running to first
base. While I was running I could just feel the blood coming out of my
rectum. They took me out of the game and took me to the hospital. I
had had all of these tests already and they didn't find anything, but there
was something wrong.

More tests followed and then I went back to playing again. A few
days later we traveled to Sendai where there was a doctor who was a specialist. I was having terrific stomach pain and bleeding. The specialist
put me into some kind of contraption for a test that turned me upside-
down, and he finally found it. I had colon cancer. This was in August,
about three-quarters of the way through the season.

When the diagnosis was made, everyone around me was all sad
and worried and was acting like I was going to die. I said, "OK,
what are we going to do now? What are we supposed to do?" I was pretty
calm about it, considering. I felt that I was in the middle of the best
season I ever had on the field so I couldn't be too far gone. It wasn't
affecting my play at all. I was hitting .356 and leading the league in

home runs and RBI, so I thought whatever was wrong with me couldn't be too bad.

Of course I knew that cancer could be fatal and that sometimes just hearing the word itself scared a lot of people. The people around me in Japan were very fatalistic when they heard the diagnosis. The manager, who was the famous 400-game-winner Masaichi Kaneda, the coaches, and the people with the team, started acting like it was the end of the world. They acted like it was contagious. I just wanted to deal with it and fix the problem.

I called a friend back in Chicago and he said he would ask around to find the best specialist, the best surgeon. There were people connected to the Orions who were thinking I would have the operation in Tokyo, but my friend said, "No, come back here because I've got a guy who is renowned." Also, I knew about Lou Jackson passing in Japan and that concerned me, so I said that I was going back to the States. When I went back to Chicago for surgery in late August, I felt that no one in Tokyo ever expected to see me again. Everyone there, from the players on up, had a doom and gloom attitude about it. When they first found out, even in front of me they were going, "Aw, man," and "aw, gee." Anybody who heard about it, they all had the end-of-the-world outlook.

Some days I thought I was the only one who believed I was going to live. I don't know why I was so relaxed about it after being told I had colon cancer, but for some reason I thought this too shall pass. I just thought it couldn't be too bad because I was playing so well. There were some scary things, though, because there was blood when I went to the bathroom. I just felt it would get better by cutting the cancer out. My attitude has always been to think positively, especially if there are things you can't control. I didn't know of any history of cancer in my family, either, though at the time I didn't even know who my paternal grand-father was. I later found out there is a significant amount of cancer on that side of the family.

I flew back in late August and registered at Northwestern Hospital in Chicago. The operation lasted several hours and I stayed in the hospital for a while to recuperate. In those days they didn't throw you out of the hospital as fast as they could, so I was in there for some time. Then I recuperated in Chicago.

When I went in for surgery I went into the hospital with the idea that my friend had gotten the best doctor, and I knew Northwestern had a good reputation. It was a great hospital. The doctors told me if they caught the cancer early enough that it should be okay, though we would have to monitor it for five years to make sure it didn't come back. Jim Lefebvre told me his father had the same thing 20 years earlier and was still kicking.

The doctors did catch the cancer early. They said it hadn't spread to the lymph nodes. I wasn't scared at all before the operation. There's only one thing that can happen if it doesn't work and that's die. You can't do anything about it, so why worry? If worry would have helped, I'd have done it.

I stayed in the hospital almost two weeks, but part of that was because I contracted pneumonia. I stayed in the recuperation room a long time and it was very cold in there. Because of fear of infection they kept it at something like 40 degrees. That was the worst part of my time in the hospital, getting inhalation therapy to get all that stuff out of my lungs. They try to make you cough that stuff up. That was terrible.

When I woke up I got the good news that the doctors got all of the cancer. I was definitely weak. My friend told me that when the doctors came out from surgery they said, "Boy, it was big." My friend said that for a while he was worried.

We were in first place when I left Japan by quite a few games, and the Orions ended up winning that year. We won the whole thing. After I regained my strength in Chicago I flew back to Tokyo to be part of the celebration. Probably a month had passed since they saw me. Part of the reason that I went back, besides to take part in the festivities, was to negotiate a contract for the next year. When I left, everyone thought I was going to die and they were never going to see me again, so I thought it was important to show my face and show everyone that I looked pretty good and was still going to be around. I'm not sure the team thought I was going to be able to play again, but they invited me back to attend the banquet celebration.

I was still somewhat weak and I had lost a lot of weight, so it wasn't as if I looked like I could take the field right away. When I went back I made it clear I wanted to play again the next year. I was completely committed to playing the next season. The Orions still had Jim Lefebvre under contract and they gave him big bucks. I think the manager,

Kaneda, wanted to sign another American and have me around as coach, and just have me as an insurance policy if something happened to one of the other foreign players. In some ways that wouldn't have been so bad, but I was 42 and I didn't have that much time left. I may have been at less than full strength, but I had to get back in shape to play the next year because of my pledge to continue playing until I had a sub-par year.

My relationship with Kaneda in Tokyo was like the relationship between Ernie Banks and Leo Durocher on the Cubs, not good. He was a retired superstar player who was only 38, and I was over 40. He was trying to figure out why I'm still playing and he can't still play at that age. As a matter of fact, he pissed off a lot of hitters during batting practice. He tried to get everybody out during batting practice instead of just letting the hitters bat. He still thought he could get everybody out and that was his forum to show it. Anyway, after the surgery, when it came time to talk about a contract, he wanted to release me. Then he said, "I'll tell you what, you take a 50 percent pay cut and come back as a coach." I said, "Wait a minute. No, I don't think so."

Kaneda wanted to cut my salary to the bone and just pay me a coach's salary. I felt I could still play. Until I got sick I was having my best year of all, so why wouldn't I think I could still play? I had led that team in practically every offensive category for years and still wasn't paid as much as Jim, who was struggling every year. Everything was still coming easy. I felt I had everything figured out. I went to Tokyo, took part in the celebration, but left Japan without a contract for the next year. They had an offer on the table to me and it wasn't satisfactory.

I heard that some other teams had inquired about my availability, but Kaneda had his own scheme working to force me into being a coach with the Orions and didn't want anyone else to have me. He said terrible things about me in the newspaper. He said nobody should sign me to play because it would be detrimental to my health. He said that if I played it might hasten my death and stuff like that. It was all B.S.

Essentially, I was a free agent, free to sign with any team in Japan, or any team anywhere else in the world. I didn't need that kind of stuff going on with Kaneda. But he scared a lot of teams away from me. They didn't want to take a chance on me. They knew I had been sick and they believed what Kaneda said in the papers. Finally, the Hanshin Tigers in the Central League contacted me and said they were interested. They had just released Willie Kirkland and the team went 1–4 in the spring exhibition season. They were willing to sign me if I took a physical and proved I was healthy enough to play. They were definitely scared by the illness, but they were willing to check it out. I took the physical and it showed I was fine, and they signed me.

People in Japan are terrified of cancer. It scares them. I became a Tiger and I went back to Japan. I had to show everyone I was okay. I'd been working out so I was getting sharper, and the reporters came out to see me at the field just before spring training. It was either late January or early February, a few months after the surgery and recuperation.

When I first returned to Tokyo I still had my same apartment, and I did a lot of working out on my own on the roof. So before I joined the team I knew I had pretty good stamina. It wasn't as good as my top conditioning from say, five years earlier, but I thought I was in pretty good shape. Eventually, I gave up my apartment in Tokyo and moved to Osaka. I moved in with another American player, Clarence Jones. Jones was another former Cub and he hit it big in Japan. In 1974, he became the first foreign player to lead the Pacific League in home runs. He hit 38 homers for the Kintetsu Buffaloes that year. He won the home run crown again in 1976 with 36 homers. He did well for himself in Japan. Officially, spring training hadn't started, but I would go out to this park and train in Osaka. These reporters came out to see how I was doing, so I went running for an hour and a half. It may have seemed as if I was training to run the Boston Marathon and not play baseball in Osaka, but I wanted to show them how great I was doing. It worked. These stories came out in the newspapers that I was doing okay. The publicity helped me and it made everyone stop worrying about me. But I'll tell you, after that run, my legs felt like stilts. I could hardly walk.

The important thing was that I proved a point and showed people I was still around. Hanshin signed me to play first base instead of the outfield, which was interesting because I hadn't played first for a couple of years. Hanshin was a good team. The Tigers had some terrific players. Hanshin was the next best team in the Central League behind Yomiuri.

Even after the colon cancer, the surgery, the recuperation and being weak for a while, I started off the season tremendously again. In some ways I may have started off too good. I hit two home runs, one a grand slam, and had a four-hit game on opening day on the road. I think I scared the whole league because teams stopped pitching to me. And the umpires came into it again. It was just hard dealing with that strike zone thing again. They feared that I would threaten Oh for batting supremacy at 42 years of age.

But worse than that, I started to feel fatigued. I had the great start and that was exhilarating, but then I hit a patch where I was hitting balls all over the place, hitting balls on the nose, but they weren't carrying as far. I think my body was weaker than I thought and that I needed more time to regain my strength. I probably needed more time than I took to bulk up again after losing weight. Hanshin had adopted the same kind of rigorous training that

During his final season playing in Japan, in 1975, George Altman was 42 years old and competing for the Hanshin Tigers. He had just beaten colon cancer, and proved he could still play.

Kaneda was using with the Orions because it worked and they won the championship. We were running three or four miles before practice, and instead of the hard work building me up, it was wearing me down. I could tell that I was not as strong as I usually was. I was feeling the lingering effects of the chemotherapy. Anyone who has undergone chemotherapy knows what I am talking about.

Hanshin's ballpark was different, too. It was a lot bigger park than I had been playing in with Tokyo and the winds were different. The wind was against me, blowing in from right field. I can remember hitting a lot of balls out there and they just died. They'd get to the warning track and die. I thought if I had a little more time to get a little bit stronger I could have had a really good year. Instead, I ended up batting .274. That's when I decided it was time to quit.

My average had declined. For whatever reason, the illness or age, I was no longer a .300 hitter. There were several factors. I switched from the Pacific League to the Central League and I didn't know the pitchers as well. In that league it was ingrained that no one was going to be able to hit like Sadarahu Oh or Shigeo Nagashima. If anyone got too hot or challenged their records or averages, they would just get pitched around.

It was very satisfying to be able to come back and play one more year after being diagnosed with colon cancer and play as well as I did. I got baseball out of my system by doing that. I was 42 and one day there was an article that said the players on opposing teams were going to attack me on defense at first base by bunting. They tried, but I could still move and that didn't work so well. But it did feel like it was the right time to retire. I graduated college in 1955 and I stopped playing in 1975, so it had been 20 years.

Looking back at that time in Japan so many years ago, I'm really glad that I got the opportunity to play there. It was very important to me. I would really have been disappointed if my baseball career had ended with the Cubs. I didn't think I had the kind of major league career I should have had. There were unfortunate circumstances and injuries, but part of my mind said, "That's just an excuse." Another part of my mind said that if I had been healthy I would have had more great years in the majors. By going to Japan and having those good years I could think, "Aha, that's what I thought. I could still play." I had that satisfaction.

I had a lot of good experiences. I met a lot of good people. I gained patience. I developed more humility. I learned to become a better hitter, too, because in the states I was relying strictly on ability, whatever natural talent I had. But with all of the batting practice over in Japan I learned how to hit, what my strengths were, and how to play to my strengths. I learned how to handle the bat differently.

Something else I picked up on that helped me was watching one of the other best hitters in Japan play pepper for five minutes at the end of his pre-game preparation as a regular part of his warm-up. I started doing that and it improved my bat control. It improved my contact. I didn't strike out nearly as much. I said if I was ever coaching a team I would go back to the old days where players played pepper all of the time. Players today don't do it nearly as often. Maybe it's because they get in the way of the groundskeepers right before a game. Maybe it's because players always do it on the sidelines close to the stands and they're afraid of the liability if they hit anyone. But I think it's a very good thing for bat control.

One of the things I also picked up by spending eight baseball seasons in Japan was some of the language. I was never fluent, but even after 40 years I can still remember some words, like a few baseball terms, like hello, how's the family. It's not as if I get a chance to use Japanese in everyday life now. I've forgotten a lot of Japanese, but if I ran into a Japanese speaker I think some of it would come back.

I always had an interesting time with the players when they were trying to speak English, too. One guy was trying to say some things in English around the batting cage once. He kept saying "onion cob, onion cob." I was trying to understand him and was saying, "What the hell is an onion cob?" He was trying to tell the batting practice pitcher to throw him only curveballs. Onion cob, only curve.

After all of these years I still do stay in touch with some guys in Japan. We write letters. Of all people, I get cards from Kaneda every year. I guess he was feeling remorseful about how he treated me at the end of my career with Tokyo. So I hear from Masaichi Kaneda. Who would have guessed? He even came to Chicago and we had a nice and cordial visit. I can't say he came specifically to visit me, but it was nice to see him again and mend fences.

21

Retirement

Most athletes hope that they can make enough money during their playing days so they don't ever have to work again. In the modern age of professional sports, with even back-up players earning salaries that can reach into the millions of dollars and every single player in every major sport earning six-figure salaries, that is not a far-fetched scenario.

In the 1950s, 1960s, and into the 1970s, that was a privilege according to only a select few. During that era of pro sports, most athletes had to hold down off-season jobs to make ends meet and to support their families, never mind after retirement. Once a sports figure retired from his game he might try to stay in the sport as a coach or manager, but the most retiring athletes had to seek out another career.

Many athletes sought to trade on their well-known names and parlay their fame into a fresh career. It might be establishing a restaurant, selling insurance, obtaining a car dealership, or going into business.

After he recovered from the scary bout with cancer, George Altman moved on to his next career. He invested $140,000 and bought a seat on the Chicago Board of Trade. Altman had earned a college degree from Tennessee State two decades earlier when he believed he might become a teacher or high school coach. In the years that followed he became more interested in the business world.

Long before, Altman had studied for his stock broker's license and obtained it, so becoming a stock broker was one option. He considered all types of businesses. He had dabbled in various types of off-season work. He was always conscious of the fact that he was going to have to work in the civilian world once he finished playing baseball. He was in no hurry to give up the game, but when he finally did he was closing in on his 43rd birthday.

I was at peace when I retired from baseball. The time had come to do something else. I didn't miss baseball when I retired. I played for 20 years after college. I never coached anywhere. I had a little bit of pride and I felt that if somebody wanted me, in a winter league, anywhere, or any team, I would help, but they would have to approach me. I had the satisfaction of knowing that I did all I could in the sport despite some setbacks, and now that I was healthy again after colon cancer surgery in 1976 I was ready to begin a new life.

The first thing I had in mind was to look into buying a McDonald's franchise. I had saved some money, and going back to the early 1960s Ernie Banks had become friendly with the founder of McDonald's, Ray Kroc. Ray Kroc eventually owned the San Diego Padres from 1974 to 1984, but Ernie met him when we were playing for the Cubs. He said, "One day you'll say, 'I know Ray Kroc.'" Ernie said we could get a McDonald's franchise for something like $8,000. I said, "Hey, that's great." Ernie Banks was saying the same thing. Ernie had a lot of enthusiasm when he heard about things, but he didn't follow through. What I think happened is that we brought the idea to the Cubs' owner, P. K. Wrigley, who used to try to give that kind of business advice to players if he thought something was a good deal, and he kind of put a damper on it. He didn't think it was a great investment. We could have been very wealthy.

When I left Japan and came back to Chicago to live, the idea was still in my head about getting a McDonald's franchise. I made some inquiries, but what I discovered was that the Cubs second baseman, Glenn Beckert, was ahead of me in line and that he had actually gone to hamburger school or something. The opportunity wasn't there to get a franchise in Chicago because if there was going to be a new one, Beckert would probably get it.

McDonald's actually did offer me the opportunity for a franchise in a small town outside of Chicago, but I decided not to do it. That's when I returned to my idea of becoming a stock broker. I was at a party with a friend of mine who worked at the Chicago Board of Trade. I told him that I wanted to reactivate my stock broker's license and become a stock broker. But I indicated to him that I was worried about losing money for other people because whatever stocks you recommend, it's a reflection on you. If an investment went bad I would feel badly about it.

He thought about what I said and he said maybe I should look into the Board of Trade because I'd be working on my own account and investing for myself right on the floor. My reaction was, "Oh yeah?" I wanted to be in the investment business, but I didn't want to lose money for other people. I didn't want to lose money for me, either, but I would feel better if the responsibility was all on me with my own money. My friend said, "Come on down and look at it."

I did take a trip down there and went on the floor. It was pretty wild. There was chaos in the room, guys pushing and shoving and screaming. I talked to one of the successful brokers there and he showed me this card and how it made him $400 that hour. He said an interesting thing, too, that my size — how tall I was — would be an advantage on the floor because it would enable me to be seen and heard. Of course I was fairly soft-spoken and you had to yell on the floor. I was always able to do what I had to do.

After my visit to the Board of Trade I thought it over and decided to give it a try. I wasn't too happy about having to pay $140,000 to get a job, though. That's how much it cost to buy a seat on the exchange. I had managed to save that much cash from my playing days, and I put down most of it and saved another $30,000 for trading capital. I set up my own account. Before the end of 1976 I was working at the Chicago Board of Trade as a commodities trader. I did that for 13 years, just representing myself.

It's really a tragedy that so many athletes don't plan ahead for retirement. The athlete has a certain advantage because he has contacts and can develop them while he's playing. Because after you're finished, they forget you very quickly.[21]

I worked five days a week at the Board of Trade, starting at around 7:30 A.M. and running until about 2 P.M. It was a frenzy of action. Everyone is buying, selling, yelling. Most of us were day traders. I started out buying wheat. Then I moved over to the bean pit. You'd call out a number which was like a contract to purchase 50,000 beans. That meant 50,000 bushels for wheat. If you yelled out "five" for beans that meant five lots of 10,000. You might buy a contract one minute and in the next minute you might sell it right back for a small profit. How it worked was that some of the major people would come in and buy thousands of contracts. You might buy 100 shares, or 20, or five, and sell it right back. Most of the time the increments of profit were $50 or $25, and sometimes you might lose $25 or $50. If you froze up and didn't move fast enough you could lose thousands of dollars. You had to get out from under the contract in a hurry if it started to go bad and started to work against you.

Working at the Board of Trade was like baseball to me. Each time you made a trade was like coming up to bat. You either won it or lost it. If you lost it, it was like making an out, and you just had to go on to the next one. The same thing with evaluating the whole day. Most of the time you came out ahead, hopefully, but a lot of days you're going to come out behind. Some days you might lose real big. You had to know in your mind that you would be back the next day, just like baseball. You'd go oh-for-four and know tomorrow was another day.

There was a lot of pressure. There was a period after my son was killed in that automobile accident in New Mexico when I lost my concentration while trading sometimes, and I got in a rut where I didn't trade as sharply as I had been doing it before. There was also some nepotism on the floor between individual traders. Usually the first guy with the best price made the deal. But sometimes you were ignored because they had a special guy they wanted to deal with who was a cousin or a brother to make the good trades with. I could handle that for a little while at first, but after my son was killed I got tired of it. I got a little bit older, too. Being a commodities trader is hard work. I did fairly well and I could have probably done better if I took more chances by buying 100 lots at a time instead of going for 10 or 20.

I worked conservatively. Only occasionally would I buy 50 lots of something, and very rarely did I buy 100. I wanted to be careful. Some of the young guys who came along started to trade large and busted out quick. The average trader lasts three or four years, but if you are in for the long haul you have to have discipline to keep from busting out. I couldn't afford to bust out. This was my job. This was my income. Handling it the way I did, I made more money at the Board of Trade than I did playing baseball. I was careful. I think one year I made $250,000, and I did that by being conservative.

One time I had a chance to buy silver at $4 a share and I kept waiting for a better deal and missed out. That wouldn't have been an in and out thing. I kept waiting for the price to go lower and it never did. Then silver took off and I think it went to $40. One time I invested in bonds

After retiring from baseball in the 1970s, George Altman made his living working at the Chicago Board of Trade. He bought a seat on the exchange and swiftly moved into the high-risk profession.

when they first came out and I held them and held them. I was down $40,000 when they came back and I got out. It was a lot of pressure, a lot of tension, and a lot of work. Had I held on longer to that trade, I could have netted more than $100,000.

Once I settled in and worked at the Chicago Board of Trade I got involved in youth work again, too. I had helped to start the George Altman Little League on the South Side when I played for the Cubs. Now that I had more time, I joined the board of the Woodlawn Boys Club. Our task was to raise money for the clubs and to see that the programs were run properly.

At one time while I was working at the Board of Trade, some of us helped get the New Orleans Cotton Exchange started. It had existed before and we were trying to get it going again, but we weren't able to sustain it. It was a different way for me to make money from cotton from when I was younger and had to pick it. That would have been like getting revenge on cotton for all of the hard work I went through in the hot sun.

Once I settled down in Chicago and worked at the Board of Trade I got involved in other activities in the area. Going back to when I was with the Cubs, I also helped start a chess club for young people on the West Side and get the Better Boys Foundation going. I was involved with that for 30 years or so. Every year I helped raise money for the Better Boys Foundation.

The idea was to give kids in the neighborhood something to do. The Better Boys Foundation started with a boxing program and added basketball and so forth. Eventually they dropped the boxing. Kids in the area were still getting involved in gangs and they changed the focus to educate younger kids. One of the fund-raisers we had was a banquet where the guests of honor were players who won various statistical categories in the National Football League. People bought $100 tickets for the dinner. We had it at the Hilton Hotel in Chicago. Walter Payton was there and we had the best defensive end and that kind of thing. It was a huge thing. All of the guys came.

I also got involved with organizations that worked against drug abuse in Chicago and in Missouri. After I left the Board of Trade, my wife Etta wanted to go back to school and we moved to Jefferson City, Missouri, so she could attend Lincoln University. And I got involved with an organization against drug abuse there. Being a quasi-celebrity as a baseball player, I felt I could lend my name to these groups and help them raise money.

We only planned to stay in Jefferson City for four years, but we stayed much longer, for more than a decade. Also while I lived there I became involved in a mentorship program at Jefferson City High School. We worked with at-risk kids who were having problems at school and stuff like that, trying to keep them straight.

One of the kids that I mentored there was 16 years old when he transferred in from Los Angeles. He was a pretty decent kid, but he got in trouble, running around with three adults, and they were charged with trying to abort a fetus with cocaine and anti-freeze. He was only 16 and he ended up with a 30-year sentence. I thought that was an injustice to the young man and maybe a little bit of discrimination. He was African American and the others were white adults. One lady, who was the chief perpetrator, got 30 years. The other lady, who was 24 or 25, turned state's evidence against everybody else and she only got six years. The other 21-year-old guy got about 18 years. The boy is still in prison. I've been in touch with him for the last 15 years or so. We're trying to see what we can do to have the case looked at again. I still get letters from him about every month. We correspond. I go to see him once in a while and I'm amazed at how he's held up in that situation. It's a shame. I have seen murderers sentenced to less time by the courts.

Just about all of the organizations that I have worked with have focused on helping high school-aged kids. We see so many kids that go wayward and go to prison. Some of them are just children that end up in prison. You just feel that you have an obligation to see what you can do to get them to stay in school, stay away from drugs, and maybe steer them to sports instead of drugs. It's just a sad, sad thing. What happened to my grandson Jonas is an example of the types of things kids can face.

Jonas was my daughter's son. He was 16 years old and visiting a friend in Chicago in another part of the city from where he lived. This kid supposedly found a gun in the trash — this is supposedly — and he carried this gun around with him all day, a .22-caliber semi-automatic. My grandson was with this kid all day. They were out and playing. He was getting ready to go home about 10 o'clock at night and this kid, who is 14, pulls out the gun. He's supposedly showing it around and he pointed it at Jonas and the gun went off. Laura, my daughter, said the bullet hit him in the neck and he bled to death. I lost a grandson that way. I lost my son George Jr. in an auto accident. My daughter was very protective of Jonas. She didn't let him run around unsupervised. He only played with kids he knew and still this happened. When Jonas died we asked that people honor his memory by giving contributions to the Hands Without Guns/Help For Survivors organization. That group provides support for families that lost loved ones to gun violence.

Losing a son, losing a grandson, it was really, really hard. You never get over it. I was never really sure about it being an accident with my grandson. Why, if a kid carried the gun around all day, would he wait all that time to show it? I just think it's unbelievable that these things happen. I wondered if it was a gang initiation, or something, that maybe it happened on purpose. You can't prove it. The other kid said it was an accident. He said he didn't know the gun was loaded. He was sorry, but he actually didn't show a lot of remorse and he got something like four or five years as a sentence. That happened in 1999. My son's accident was about 13 years before that. You feel that you try to do what you can to help prevent kids from going through these things.

The only baseball coaching I ever did after I retired was at Lincoln University when we were living in Missouri. They were a small college and I worked as a volunteer. It kept me in the game a little bit.

At various times I was called upon to make speeches, sometimes by charitable groups, sometimes by sports groups, sometimes for Black History Month. Some people got interested in the Negro Leagues. At one time I gave speeches fairly frequently. Now I only do one or two a year, just periodically. I've given speeches to business groups, as well, and this might not be surprising, but I often have some baseball stories involved in my speeches. I have spoken about drug abuse among young people in front of some of these groups.

One story I told was about Satchel Paige when we were with the Kansas City Monarchs. Satch and most of the veterans were hard on rookies. You really had to earn your spurs before you were accepted. Satch would often needle a rookie by walking halfway to home plate and saying, "Son, what kind of pitch would you like to miss?"

Buck O'Neil was a big influence on me and I included stories about Buck in some of my talks, too. I talked about the early days of the Negro Leagues, and the heyday between 1925 and 1948. There were some powerful teams with some amazing and colorful players. There were a lot of players with nicknames that defined their skills. Players like Joe "Bullet" Rogan, Double Duty Radcliffe, Cool Papa Bell, and George "Never" Sweatt, to name a few. In the Negro Leagues, most often the bus driver

George Altman

was the trainer. His equipment consisted of band-aids, tape, and maybe alcohol. When you got hurt and couldn't play, they sent you home, or more likely released you with no pay and you had to get home the best you could. They tell the story about a rookie that got hit in the head with a pitch. He lay down on the ground, expecting some immediate care and sympathy. After a minute the manager slowly strolled out to home plate, looked him over and said, "Boy, can you see first base?" He said yes. The manager said, "Then get up and get on it."

The veterans also said that some clubs would send a struggling player around the corner on an errand on getaway day. When he returned, his bags were sitting on the curb and the bus was long gone.

I called upon my own experience in sports in my speeches, I always tried to tell a little bit about the Negro Leagues, and I was always on the lookout for good sayings that I could fit in and use in my talks. Notre Dame football coach Lou Holtz had a list of "10 Commandments For Success," and I mentioned those a lot. Some of the things on his list do sound like the commandments, such as "Care About People." The item he ranked as No. 1 was "Do Right." And No. 2 was "Do Your Best." I believed in all of those things.

Any time I could find things that I thought were interesting, informative, or amusing, I might use the material. There was a joke I told sometimes about Little Johnny in a kindergarten class that went on a field trip to the police station. The kids saw pictures tacked to the bulletin boards and one of the youngsters asked if they were really the most wanted criminals. The policemen told the kids that yes they were and they very much wanted to capture them. Little Johnny asked, "Why didn't you keep him when you took his picture?"

After a few seasons, when I was still playing with the Cubs, I was invited back home to Goldsboro, North Carolina, and they gave me a key to the city. There was a little parade to celebrate the occasion, too. There was satisfaction in that, to be remembered. To me the town seemed the same that it had always been even though I had been away for years. Nothing much happens down there. There wasn't much progress. The difference for me is that I came back as a star and a celebrity. It's always nice to be recognized by your roots.

In 1989, I was invited back to Goldsboro to be inducted into the community's sports Hall of Fame, and that was pretty neat. I got a nice plaque as a souvenir. I still have some relatives there. One of the other local athletes inducted with me also made his career in professional baseball, Jerry Narron. Jerry played in the majors for eight years with four teams, starting in 1979. He is a lot younger than me.

Another of the people inducted into the Goldsboro Hall of Fame with me was the basketball player Mike Evans. Mike is a second or third cousin of mine. He was a high school basketball star in Goldsboro and he got a basketball scholarship to play at Kansas State. He was the first person from Wayne County to reach the NBA, and he played with the San Antonio Spurs, the Milwaukee Bucks, a couple of other teams, and then played in Europe. He was like me in that sense. He extended his career by going to a foreign country.

Donna Atkinson, who was a star basketball player and played at Vanderbilt, then played professionally, was also my cousin. There were three African Americans in the class of inductees and we were all related. That was pretty special and something pretty unusual.

It was a nice ceremony. They filled up the hall they had there in the school auditorium. A lot of my old coaches were there, some of my teammates from the old days. They sat with me at my table at the dinner. It was a great evening. I'd been going home every three or four years, but this was something else.

One of the things about going back to Goldsboro for the Hall of Fame event that demonstrated things were different than they had been when I was growing up was that everything was integrated. In fact, the school auditorium was in the white high school that I didn't even know where it was when I was living there. That was a little bit ironic. I thought about that some when I was there. There was sportswriter named Jack Lee in town that came along and kept up with my career when I was with the Cubs and afterwards. I saw him whenever I came home. He kept all of the local fans up to date about what I was doing. He was a big fan.

Given the intensity of my interest in keeping kids off drugs and alcohol and out of trouble, it shouldn't be surprising that I also wrote a poem that I sometimes used in my talks, too, about the evils of substance abuse. This is how the first stanza goes:

Drugs and booze are twin Diseases
They will bring you to your knees

If you "wanna" go places in your life
You must get away from Booze, Drugs and strife
AH, PUT 'EM DOWN, AH PUT 'EM DOWN, PUT 'EM DOWN, PUT
'EM DOWN, PUT 'EM DOWN, PUT 'EM DOWN."

Then came:

I had a friend John. He was a fool
All his pals were dealing in crack
I said, John Boy, you better come back
My advice to him was sound
PUT 'EM DOWN, PUT 'EM DOWN, PUT 'EM DOWN, PUT 'EM
DOWN."
Put 'em down, put 'em down is good advice
If your head is clear you wouldn't think twice
You would know it's true and straight from the heart
But the best remedy is never to start
PUT 'EM DOWN, PUT 'EM DOWN, PUT 'EM DOWN, PUT 'EM
DOWN."
John wanted to be rich real fast
Knowing all the time it would never last
He rode through town in a big Mercedes
Though he was young he was big with the ladies
He sold and smoked crack whenever he could
All my friends said I definitely should
PUT 'EM DOWN, PUT 'EM DOWN, PUT 'EM DOWN, PUT 'EM
DOWN."

The last stanza goes like this:

Just last week it all came to a head
Gang warfare and friend John was dead
His funeral was the biggest in town
The last thing said ... PUT 'EM DOWN, PUT 'EM DOWN.
Now if you are on dope and you want to have hope
Don't frown!
PUT 'EM DOWN, PUT 'EM DOWN, PUT 'EM DOWN, PUT 'EM
DOWN."

You can tell how strongly I felt about this issue by the way I poured
my thoughts into the poem.

22

Quite a Life in Baseball

George Altman was an All-Star, but not a long-term superstar in major league baseball, spreading his allegiance around between the Chicago Cubs, the St. Louis Cardinals and the New York Mets.

He spent the majority of his nine-year big-league career with the Cubs, but in retirement he lives in the suburbs of St. Louis. He watches Cardinals games on television often, along with other sporting events, and he attends a handful of Cardinals home games a year. He roots harder for the Cubs, though, even though he wasn't at all unhappy when St. Louis won the 2011 World Series.

Just like the legion of Cubs fans that still begin each spring with optimism that their beloved team will finally win its first World Series soon after an intermission of more than 100 years since 1908, Altman would love to see Chicago capture another World Series in his lifetime.

He owns souvenirs of his playing days, especially photographs of him wearing all of the uniforms representing the teams that he played for, and former teammates and friends he made along the way. These include newspaper articles from Japan — in the English language Japan Times and in Japanese language periodicals where the headlines are gigantic, but also indecipherable to someone that doesn't speak the language.

Now in his mid–70s, Altman is most definitely retired from playing any type of baseball, but one of his later-in-life-passions, as he stays trim, is competing at horseshoes. He admits that he brings the same competitive nature to horseshoes as he did to basketball and baseball when he was much younger.

Residing in a pleasant subdivision outside of St. Louis with wife Etta, who is a part-time piano teacher, Altman says his most prized possessions may be the memories from his baseball days. He got to see the country for sure, and he saw and became intimate with another part of the world through the sport. And until he hears differently from an unknown contender, he can claim the world's championship for playing baseball at more levels (the big three being the majors, the Negro Leagues and Japan) than any other human being who ever wore a glove.

I have not often thought about my career being unique, with stops in Japan, Cuba, Panama, college, the Army, the minors, the majors, and the Negro Leagues, because each time I signed on to play for one of the teams in those places I was just going where the game took me.

Timing had a lot to do with it, too. The Negro Leagues were coming to an end, and if I was any younger I wouldn't have experienced the full-fledged team aspect and the standings in that league. Getting drafted into the Army was not something I could control, but I ended up getting the opportunity to play baseball there instead of being shipped to a jungle to fight a war. The winter ball opportunities took me where the games were, and if I had come along a little bit later I never would have played in Cuba.

I will say that it's ironic that I felt more relaxed playing baseball outside of the United States in Panama, Cuba and Japan. It's like there was no pressure. I don't know why, but I just felt that way. It might have been connected to the fact that I came from the segregated south and in the United States I was playing against Caucasians, which I wasn't used to at first. I probably subconsciously believed that you had to play a little bit better than the white players, or else you would get cut.

There was pressure to perform in Japan, too, when you were one of only two foreigners on the team. You had to produce quickly or you would get sent home early. They weren't going to carry you on the roster if you didn't do well. But you didn't feel it as a social burden there. In Japan once, we got to meet the prime minister in his office in the capital. That's one of the things that come along as a perk when you play baseball and your team wins, especially if the prime minister is a fan of your team.

I am definitely proud of the career that I had. Japan turned into a wonderful experience for developing character and confidence. It is interesting that if I hadn't had the injuries in the majors and the disappointments, I never would have gone there. It was a case of an opportunity presenting itself at a time of adversity and me being able to take advantage of it.

Being the right age also gave me the opportunity to play for the Kansas City Monarchs. If I was any younger I would have missed out and that would have been a shame. It was a very enriching experience. I played with veterans of the game, older black men who had been through a lot. I saw first-hand that those guys had talent. They were older, at the end of their careers, and I was younger and just starting out. One of the Monarch veterans, Hank Baylis, took me aside and said, "I think you can make the major leagues. You've got enough talent to make the majors, and I've seen a lot of players come through here. I think you're one of the better ones." Stuff like that coming from veteran players who had seen it all really boosted my confidence.

I was fortunate that I got to play that year because it forever linked me with the Negro Leagues. There were still teams barnstorming after 1955, but my year was the last year they kept track of wins and losses in the standings. It wouldn't have been the same. Because I played that one year, I have been invited to participate in a lot of events. In 2004, the Negro Leagues Baseball Museum in Kansas City invited me to participate in an oral history project where they were tape recording stories from all of the Negro Leagues players who were still alive.

At other times I was asked to make speeches about what the Negro Leagues were like. Even counting 1960 as the end point, that's more than half a century ago, so there are a lot of baseball fans who don't know anything about it, why the leagues existed, and the younger fans don't know about the discrimination keeping African Americans out of the majors. In December of 2010, I spoke to a symposium promoting diversity that was sponsored by Coors and Miller, the beer people. I talked about Buck O'Neil a lot and mentioned the names of some of the best players like Satchel Paige and the great hitting catcher, Josh Gibson. It's important that the names of the players not be forgotten. My one-year connection to the Kansas City Monarchs was very important in my life. I keep coming back to it. I own a Monarchs baseball cap that I wear around.

One year Bell South, the telephone company, put on a special event in Atlanta to honor as many Negro Leagues players as they could. There was somewhere between 60 and 75 of us there. Hank Aaron was there.

I got to spend some time with Monte Irvin. Monte was a big star in the Negro Leagues, but had his career interrupted by World War II. Monte had a good career with the New York Giants, too, and he is in the Hall of Fame. When I was a kid, Jackie Robinson and Monte Irvin were my idols. Monte is a real nice guy, a prince of a guy. We — African Americans — were mostly Dodgers fans because of Jackie Robinson. When I was in school, the principal used to have World Series games piped into the classrooms on the PA system when Brooklyn was in them. Jackie Robinson made black America into Dodgers fans. It was just like when Joe Louis fought and he was the heavyweight champion. We all listened on the radio.

The military and baseball, sports in general, were the greatest agents of change in this country when it came to race. Jackie Robinson was even active when he was still with the Monarchs. There is a story I've heard that I tell when I talk about the Negro Leagues. Back when Jackie and the team were riding through the South to a game, they stopped at a gas station. They needed to fill up and some of the players needed to use the rest room. Their gas tank was huge, holding maybe 40 gallons, so it was going to be a big sale. But the owner wouldn't let the players into the men's room. Jackie yelled, "Take the hose out of that tank." The guy probably wasn't going to sell that much gas in the next couple of months. The owner said, "OK, OK, wait a minute. You can use the rest room — but don't stay too long." What I added to that story in my speech is that "If you look at the loss of money, it is more painful than the loss of segregation." Money talks. Buck O'Neil was a master at telling this story.

I look back over my career, and not many people can say that they played with Buck O'Neil, Satchel Paige, Ernie Banks, Lou Brock, Billy Williams, Bob Gibson, and Stan Musial, and I played in the same outfield in an All-Star game with Willie Mays and Hank Aaron. Then in Japan I played against some of the greatest players in the history of that country, like Sadaharu Oh and Shigeo Nagashima.

For some reason, when I was playing winter ball in Cuba they televised a lot of games back to the states. For some reason, speaking of timing, whenever the camera was on I seemed to hit a home run. Later, some guys were telling me, "Man, you must have been Babe Ruth down there!"

Wherever I played, in the United States and other countries, one thing on my side was my competitive nature. Even when I retired from baseball, I still had that going for me. You'd better believe it that working at the Chicago Board of Trade as a commodities trader was competitive. I used to play racquetball to stay in shape and I was still competing at that. You let it out, you release the tension by taking it out on the ball. I stopped playing racquetball, though, after I tore a rotator cuff. Someone asked me if it was harder to hit the curve ball or make money in the commodities market. It's six of one and half a dozen of the other. When I gave up racquetball I took up horseshoes for competition and to stay in shape. It requires you to do a lot of walking. I do a lot of three- or four-hour practice sessions.

Once, when I was working in the commodities market, I got a chance to return to Japan. They rolled out the red carpet for me. They remembered me as a baseball player, but I went there as a trader. I was asked to talk about business. One company brought me in to talk to employees as part of their training. It had nothing to do with baseball. That company ended up with offices in Japan and Chicago.

Another time I was back in Japan later I did watch a game. It was Oh's team, the one he was managing, and I went into the Giants clubhouse and got to talk to him for a little bit. They all remembered me there. It is something to see a Japanese star like Ichiro in the United States. I think he will end up in the Hall of Fame in Cooperstown. The guy was getting 200 hits a year. If you ever saw him in Seattle at the park before a game, he had that same workout ethic and long pre-game practice routine that they observe with Japanese teams. He was always running and exercising before batting practice. He may have learned it by growing up in the game with that outlook in Japan, but he was doing it by himself once he got to the majors. That's the mindset of all the coaches and teams in Japan.

I have a lot of good baseball memories. I met a lot of good people. You hear about those boxing stories where a guy who never got to fight for the title says, "I coulda been a contender." Well, I feel I could have been a star in the major leagues, but things worked out pretty well in another way. I did okay. I was an All-Star in the majors and I was an All-Star in Japan many times, but I wasn't really a star in the United States. My lifetime batting average was .269. I was a star briefly in the States.

Probably my greatest day in the majors was hitting the two home runs off Sandy Koufax in one game and playing well in that All-Star game we won. In Japan I was a member of one Tokyo team that won the Japanese World Series. We won divisional titles in the Pacific League and we got to the World Series three other times. We lost to the Yomiuri Giants, the people's choice, all three times. Oh and Shigeo Nagashima beat us. They may have had the better team, but they also had everything going for them, from experience to momentum and the fans.

Some days it felt as if it was almost as difficult to understand the way things were done in Japanese baseball — like that strike zone thing — as it was to understand the language. And Japanese is not easy to learn. When I knew I was going there I bought a book called "Berlitz Japanese Book One." I still have it. I liked the quickie definitions of single words or single phrases in the front of the book, but that didn't mean I mastered the language. It's just like people from foreign countries who have studied English. They think they know the language, but when you talk to them it's like pidgin English or their accent is very thick. That was me in Japan. If there were any baseball words or phrases in the book, I didn't know it. There were things in there that named individual kinds of food or had sentences so you could ask, "Where's the post office?" It didn't take much

Once he gave up baseball, George Altman took up a new sport — racquetball — and competed in that sport for about two decades. He then switched his focus to horseshoes.

190

genius to figure out how to order rice in a restaurant. I ate quite a bit of rice. In Japan rice was a substitute for bread, and I had been a pretty good bread eater. They had rice for breakfast, lunch and dinner.

One funny thing that happened in Japan, going way back to when I signed with the team, was that when they were wooing me to come they said there would be another foreigner on the team. They said it would be Hector Lopez coming from the Yankees. Only it ended up that they signed Arturo Lopez. This Lopez did very well playing for Nicaragua in the Latin American Series and the Dominican Republic. He was in the Yankees' minor league system. So it was the wrong Lopez from the Yankees. Hector had more power, was a pretty good long-ball hitter, and was a veteran player. It turned out really well, though, because Arturo hit around .300 in Japan and we were teammates for four years.

One home run that I hit in the majors stands out in my mind. We were playing against the Phillies when they had Richie Allen, and he hit a 500-foot home run over the wall. Then I got into the batter's box against Chris Short and I hit one over the scoreboard which was about equally high and went for the same distance. Another time I hit a home run off of Billy Loes when he was with the Giants that went well over 400 feet. I always seem to remember hitting those long ones off the left-handers. I hit pretty well against Cincinnati all of the time, even when they had guys like Bob Purkey and Joey Jay at their best. It didn't matter.

Although I didn't save balls and bats from the majors, I saved things from Japan. But I have a Cubs uniform. It wasn't one of the ones I played in because they always wanted them back in those days. But later I got one. I do have a bat from the All-Star game in 1961, the one I hit the home run with. I still have a Willie Mays bat, too.

It's interesting that even though I have been out of the big leagues since the late 1960s, I still get a bunch of mail from collectors who send me my baseball card in stamped, self-addressed envelopes asking me to autograph them. I think I average three or four of them a day. Some days I get more, some days I get less. Fans still find me and they still write to me. I'm a little bit surprised because I haven't played in so long. Most of them say that their father saw me play and told them about me. Some say, "I wish I could have seen you play." A lot of them know my statistics and everything.

Since I retired a long time ago and had another whole career after playing baseball, I kind of downplay my days playing baseball when I go out. Etta is like my public relations person. She keeps bringing it up and telling people. It's kind of embarrassing a lot of times when she tells people I played Major League baseball. I tell her, "That and $2 will get you a cup of coffee."

I guess I downplay it too much. I suppose it's still special. It's still one of the American dreams to grow up and play Major League baseball. For me, it was good while it lasted. Now it's over. I always want to go on to something else. Now I'm competing through horseshoes. I play chess once in a while, too, against the computer. And I play poker online, free poker. I did start off playing penny ante poker on the computer, but the government stepped in and stopped that. Now I just play free poker. It's still competition.

If you played in the majors for eight years, major league baseball gives you a lifetime pass to go to games. I follow the Cubs and the Cardinals, though most of it is on TV. I don't use the pass that much. I mostly root for the Cubs. The Cardinals are my second team, so I was pulling for them when they won the 2011 World Series. It was a surprise. They were underdogs. I follow the game off the field all of the time, too. I know where free agents sign and who gets injured.

When I was doing the mentoring work in Jefferson City, one of the *St. Louis Post-Dispatch* columnists came over and wrote about me. They called me a true-blue Cubs fan, said I was a diehard Cubs fan. I do lean towards the Cubs. I'm hoping they're going to win someday while I'm still alive.

The Cubs organization and the Cardinals organizations are different animals. The Cardinals invite a lot of former players out to spring training to help with instruction. I don't see the Cubs doing that too often. The Cardinals have their winter fan convention and I go every year to sign autographs for charity. Some other players do, too. They have had the Cubs convention every winter for years and I've never been invited. I played a lot longer with the Cubs than the Cardinals. I don't like to travel too much in the winter, anyway, so I've never asked them about it. But they haven't asked me. It shows me the difference between the Cubs and the Cardinals as far as former players go. The Cardinals have a handle on their former players and we have reunions a couple of times each year. They have the guys in and they have a party. But I'm still rooting for the Cubs, still pulling for them.

You can only imagine what it will be like in Chicago if the Cubs win a World Series. It would be bedlam. There would be parades and everything. The way it looks now, it doesn't seem as if it will happen in my lifetime. Maybe Theo Epstein coming in as team president after leading the Red Sox to those World Series titles can make a difference. It will still take a long time. There were a couple of years the Cubs were right there. That time in 1984 against San Diego they were close to going to the World Series, and that time in 2003 against the Florida Marlins, with the Bartman ball, when the fan caught the foul ball, they were one game away.

Every once in a while I hear from former Cubs teammates like Cal Neeman and ex–Cardinals and even Joe Christopher, who was with the Mets. There's still some contact between the guys, and every once in a while there is some kind of reunion. Both the Cubs and the Cardinals had great fans. The Cardinals had the better organization, but if you are going to talk about loyal fans it's got to be the Cubs.

Baseball allowed me to compete and it always gave me a challenge. I think life is a bunch of challenges, and if you are able to succeed, one success leads to another and you build your confidence. You think, "Well, if I can do this, I can do other things." Baseball allowed me to make a living and compete, and it prepared me for other challenges in life.

Epilogue by Lew Freedman

Kansas City, home of the Royals of the American League, and once home of the Monarchs of the Negro Leagues, was the host of the 2012 Major League All-Star Game and its attendant hoopla, from the home run derby, to the futures game, to an extravaganza of autograph signing appearances with famous players. The game filled Kauffman Stadium, and thousands of other fans participated in peripheral festivities.

A couple of miles away, in another section of the city, a different type of baseball gathering attracted a smaller, but no less intensely interested crowd of about 200 fans. The Negro Leagues Baseball Museum conducted its own events in conjunction with the All-Star Game.

Originally, the intent was to bring together the seven living ex-players who had both participated in the Negro Leagues before the last barnstorming remnant of the operation expired in 1960 and been selected for a major league All-Star team. Old age and infirmities had reduced the number of eligible candidates and in the end held back some from traveling to the Midwest.

The magnificent seven were: Willie Mays, Ernie Banks, Monte Irvin, Hank Aaron, Don Newcombe, Minnie Minoso and George Altman. Although the group did not come together as hoped, in its stead a symposium on hitting was conducted and a storytelling session was held about the days when the Negro Leagues were the only viable big-time baseball option for young African American players with hopes.

Dave Winfield moderated a discussion that featured Aaron and Frank Robinson. All three African Americans are in the Baseball Hall of Fame. Watching attentively and mingling with the fans and other baseball figures was Altman.

Aaron clouted 755 home runs and in the early 1970s he enthralled the nation as he pursued Babe Ruth's record of 714 homers in a career. He talked of how what should have been a glorious time for him was turned into a nightmare because of death threats from racists and the need for the FBI to protect his family.

"The last two years of my career were probably the toughest of my 23 years," Aaron said of the Ruth chase. "It was kind of sad for me and it should have been joyful for me. I was merely playing baseball. I don't know where I got the strength."[22]

The large room was hushed as Aaron spilled out a tale that was publicly known, but was far more dramatic being told in his own voice. Aaron, from Mobile, Alabama, was first a member of the Indianapolis Clowns, a Negro Leagues team, before establishing his reputation with the then–Milwaukee Braves.

The Negro Leagues existed because the land of the free and the home of the brave did not permit black-skinned men to compete in major league baseball with and against white-skinned men for nearly the first half of the 20th century. Phenomenal talents like Satchel Paige, Josh Gibson, Cool Papa Bell and Buck Leonard had nowhere else to play professionally in the United States. The Negro Leagues represented a haven. Paige, the first of the black stars of the 1920s–1940s to be inducted into the Hall of Fame, was represented in the audience by a son and a daughter.

Frank Robinson did not play in the Negro Leagues before he broke into the majors as the National League "Rookie of the Year" with the Cincinnati Reds in 1956, but he was a pioneer in the game in another way. Robinson became the sport's first African American manager when he took over leadership of the Cleveland Indians in 1975.

Robinson's story, too, was well-known in this crowd, but hearing him explain details of how he became player-manager of the Indians—almost against his will — was spellbinding insider baseball. Robinson wanted to focus on playing for another year or two, and if he had he would almost certainly have reached 600 home runs and 3,000 hits, two rather elite clubs. Instead he took the reins of the big-league club and sacrificed the last days of his career.

"I wanted to further the cause for African Americans and other minorities in baseball," he said in Kansas City that day. Robinson worried that if he said no at the time, "When will that door open again?"[23]

There were other baseball figures in attendance, as well, notably Charley Pride, the pitcher-country western singer whose misfortune of a sore arm in one endeavor led to success and fame in another.

Pride was born into poverty in Sledge, Mississippi, where cotton was king and back-breaking work came with the territory unless you had a special skill to rescue you. Pride did. One of his prime motivators in pursuing a baseball career was an early fleeting thought about how it represented escape. Things went well until he hurt his elbow. Pride's goal was to end up in the Baseball Hall of Fame, but he ended up in the Country Music Hall of Fame, an example of how life paths can twist and turn.

Appropriately, during various aspects of the program, there were frequent references to Jackie Robinson. When he was accepted as a member of the Brooklyn Dodgers in 1947, Robinson became the first African American on a major league roster since the 19th century. It is well-documented that he suffered verbal abuse and threats, but comported himself with dignity and opened the doors to other blacks to play ball.

One of the event participants was Sharon Robinson, daughter of Jackie. Her mother Rachel, at 90, was still active fund-raising for various causes and speaking up about civil rights, but had a reduced travel schedule. Sharon Robinson said the family's relationship with Frank Robinson is often confused. There is none, but she jokingly referred to him as her brother. Almost as supporting evidence that the players honored in the museum represent a family, a brotherhood, Sharon Robinson said, "The Negro Leagues Museum is a treasure."[24]

The museum is located at 18th Street and Vine in Kansas City, at one time the city's hot spot for jazz and black entertainment. The area was almost a Harlem of the Midwest, and it was a big hangout for Buck O'Neil when he played for and managed the Monarchs. O'Neil used to joke that his favorite, friendly bartenders filled his glass with club soda so others would think he was partying along with them and so he could benignly people-watch.

It was through O'Neil's unflagging efforts that the museum was created in the place where it best symbolized a bygone era of Negro Leagues ball. O'Neil, one of George Altman's main mentors, died in 2006, just shy of his 95th birthday. He had become an eloquent spokesman and oral historian for the black players he knew who had preceded him in death and for the Negro Leagues in general. The charismatic O'Neil was the driving force in the establishment of the museum in 1990.

Bob Kendrick, executive director of the museum, took note of

O'Neil's overwhelming contributions to the founding of the operation and his continuing support right up until his death, noting that the museum misses O'Neil every day.

Altman and his wife Etta drove across the state from their home near St. Louis to be present for the activities. Altman was 75, but looked much younger. He sported a brown mustache and looked as trim as he had during his playing days. The weekend's worth of baseball activities was a very pleasant excursion into the past for him.

"It was a fabulous weekend," Altman said. "It was great. That was fantastic. I got to visit with Frank and Hank Aaron, and Charley Pride and some Negro Leagues players that I hadn't seen for years."

Once again Altman was reminded of just how important to his career and his heritage his one season with the Monarchs was. The connection, he said, "means everything. That's where I got my start. The three months I played with the Kansas City Monarchs; the fact that they at least took a look at me. That was the beginning. I think the museum is very important. It's like an anchor there for everybody to see.

"Hopefully, it will be there for ages. People need to know that there were terrific ballplayers back then and that they were every bit as good as the mainstream stars."

The Kansas City Monarchs opened doors for George Altman, and everywhere he played baseball (and that was just about everywhere) he proved that he was every bit as good as anyone else on the diamond.

Notes

1. Jim Auchmutey, "Players Are Gone; Memories Live On," Cox News Service, date unknown.
2. Howard Roberts, "Altman Slugging Way into Regular Job," *Chicago Daily News*, April 2, 1959.
3. Bill Traughber, "Altman Used TSU Hoop Grant to Make Big Leagues," Tennessean (Nashville), June 27, 2001. 4. Leo J. Ebenez, "Cuba Caribbean Kings for Fifth Year in Row," *The Sporting News*, February 24, 1960.
5. Bill Traughber, "Altman Used TSU Hoop Grant To Make Big Leagues," Nashville, Tennessean (Nashville), June 27, 2001.
6. Edgar Munzel, "Hats Off...!" *Chicago Tribune*, July 26, 1961.
7. Howard Roberts, "Altman Aims to Remain Healthy," *Chicago Daily News*, July 1, 1961.
8. John Kuenster, "Altman Hated to Leave," *Chicago Daily News*, October, 18, 1962.
9. Neal Russo, "Cardinals Elevate Flag Sights as Altman Gains Bat Altitude," *The Sporting News*, June 29, 1963.
10. Irving Marsh, "Mets Deal Craig to Cards for Altman," *New York Herald-Tribune*, November 5, 1963.
11. Red Smith, "Altman's a Giant in Mets' Eyes," syndicated column, *Houston Post*, November 6, 1963,
12. Ibid.
13. Joe Donnelly, "Surprise Mets Boast Major-League Hitter," *Newsday*, March 12, 1964.
14. Steve Jacobson, "The Mets Story," *Newsday*, June 26, 1964.
15. Dick Joyce, "Big George Puts Mets at Home in the Cellar," *New York World Telegram*, May 27, 1965.
16. Jerome Holtzman, "Bench Duty Helped Sharpen Altman's Eye for Clutch Hits," *Chicago Sun-Times*, November 12, 1966.
17. Eddie Gold, "Altman Found Second Wind in Far East," *Sports Collectors Digest*, date unknown, National Baseball Hall of Fame Library Archives.
18. Wells Twombley, "Big League Baseball-Japan Version," *The Sporting News*, (date missing), National Baseball Hall of Fame Library Archives.
19. Ibid.
20. Ibid.
21. "Altman Discovers Future in Soybeans," Associated Press, April 20, 1980.
22. Lew Freedman, "Hank Aaron Still Has a Story to Tell," calltothepen.com, July 12, 2012.
23. Lew Freedman, "Becoming Manager Was Sacrifice for Frank Robinson," calltothepen.com., July 13, 2012.
24. Lew Freedman, "Negro Leagues Museum a Worthy Shrine," calltothepen.com, July 8, 2012.

Index

Index

Index

Index

204

Index

Index